## More Critical Prai

### for *Nein, N*

"Mordantly funny ... Fusing provocative insights with razor-edged wit, this offers a captivating take on a haunting chapter of history."
—*Publishers Weekly*, starred review

"*Nein, Nein, Nein!* is the unbelievable true story of a guided bus tour to Nazi concentration camps, told as only Jerry Stahl can tell it, with an acid wit as deadly serious as it is hilarious, insane, and weirdly life-affirming ... Stahl is fearless, gripping, and most unsparing about his own damned soul. I read everything he writes."
—Eric Bogosian, actor/playwright

"Few have such an eye for life's perverse absurdity as Jerry Stahl ... There is nobody I'd rather take this gnarly journey with than Stahl, whose gonzo literary madness belies a steady, tender core."
—Michelle Tea, author of *Against Memoir*

"[Stahl's] razor-sharp gallows humor will have you howling one moment, breathless the next in the presence of wrenching generational pain, of humanity at its very worst, and goodness at its camouflaged best."
—*Brooklyn Rail*

"There aren't many authors today who are willing to revisit the Holocaust and write about it. But then again, most authors aren't Jerry Stahl, who has the chutzpah to pull it off masterfully ... The author's witty prose is appreciated because without levity a trip around the concentration camp horn would make any man or woman beg for mercy ... There was only one man for this job, and that man is Jerry Stahl."
—*Vol. 1 Brooklyn*

"The hallucinatory self-depreciation of Jerry Stahl's memoir allows for a nuanced look at the audacity of the ugly American ... Stahl is celebrated for his masochistic honesty that is never less than brutal and almost always on the other side of hope, but in *Nein, Nein, Nein!*, we get something dangerously close to an Anne Frank–level of optimism."
—*Texas Observer*

"An audacious, emotional journey." —*Village Voice*

"While *Nein, Nein, Nein!* is darkly confessional, it is also an exploration of how we remember the Holocaust and whether it is even possible to properly mourn and honor the victims of unspeakable tragedy ... The result is a sort of gonzo travel book about the ways the Holocaust is memorialized, commercialized, and trivialized in the countries where it took place." —*Jewish Telegraphic Agency*

"Jerry Stahl's voice is a hell-broth of fascinating contradictions: the king of mordant cool who writhes with anxious terrors, the professed nihilist with a scalding moral vision, the gifted ironist who really bleeds." —Christopher Goffard, writer/host of the podcasts *Dirty John* and *Detective Trapp*

"Stahl explores the dark side of the dark side." —Larry Charles

"There's a laugh on almost every page of *Nein, Nein, Nein,* but for all his wit and somewhat skewed perspective, Stahl never loses sight of the gravity of the places he visits ... Stahl's book shows the thought processes of a man feeling at his lowest soothing his '*shpilkes*' by experiencing one of the most sobering, draining tours one can possibly imagine." —*Jewish Journal*

"[D]aring, caustic, often laugh-out-loud manic in its staring down of Holocaust tourism." —*Moment Magazine*

"[A]ll his books showcase Stahl's lacerating humor and his talent for staring straight down the tunnel of humanity's darkest impulses ... Stahl's new memoir is no exception: Call *Nein, Nein, Nein!* a travelogue through hell, both an account of concentration camp tourism and a personal mediation on its meaning." —*Orange County Register*

"[C]rackling ... [B]izarre, distressing, hilarious, and hopeful. Read it immediately." —*CultureWag*

"Darkly hilarious ... a tour bus through literal hell ... a surreal carnival of cringe amid bursts of profound historical clarity and often unsettling emotional resonance." —Eli Valley, cartoonist, creator of *Diaspora Boy: Comics on Crisis in America and Israel*

**Jerry Stahl** is the author of ten books, including the bestsellers *Permanent Midnight*, a memoir, and the novel *I, Fatty*. His journalism has appeared in *Esquire*, the *New York Times*, *Vice*, the *Believer*, and a variety of other publications. He has written extensively for film and television, including *Hemingway & Gellhorn*, which earned a Writers Guild Award nomination, *CSI*, and *Escape at Dannemora*, for which he received an Emmy nomination.

# Nein, Nein, Nein!

One Man's Tale of Depression, Psychic
Torment, and a Bus Tour of the Holocaust

## Jerry Stahl

AKASHIC
BOOKS
BROOKLYN, NEW YORK

Note: All factual errors are entirely the author's own. Some names have been been changed, and sometimes the author hallucinates.

Published by Akashic Books
©2022, 2024 Jerry Stahl

ISBN: 978-1-63614-153-4
Library of Congress Control Number: 2021945693
First paperback printing

Akashic Books
Brooklyn, New York
Instagram, X, Facebook: AkashicBooks
E-mail: info@akashicbooks.com
Website: www.akashicbooks.com

*For Zoe Hansen*

*The world is mostly divided between madmen
who remember and madmen who forget.*
—James Baldwin

*Write books only if you are going to say in them the
things you would never dare confide to anyone.*
—E.M. Cioran

*The sky was the color of Jews.*
—Markus Zusak

# TABLE OF CONTENTS

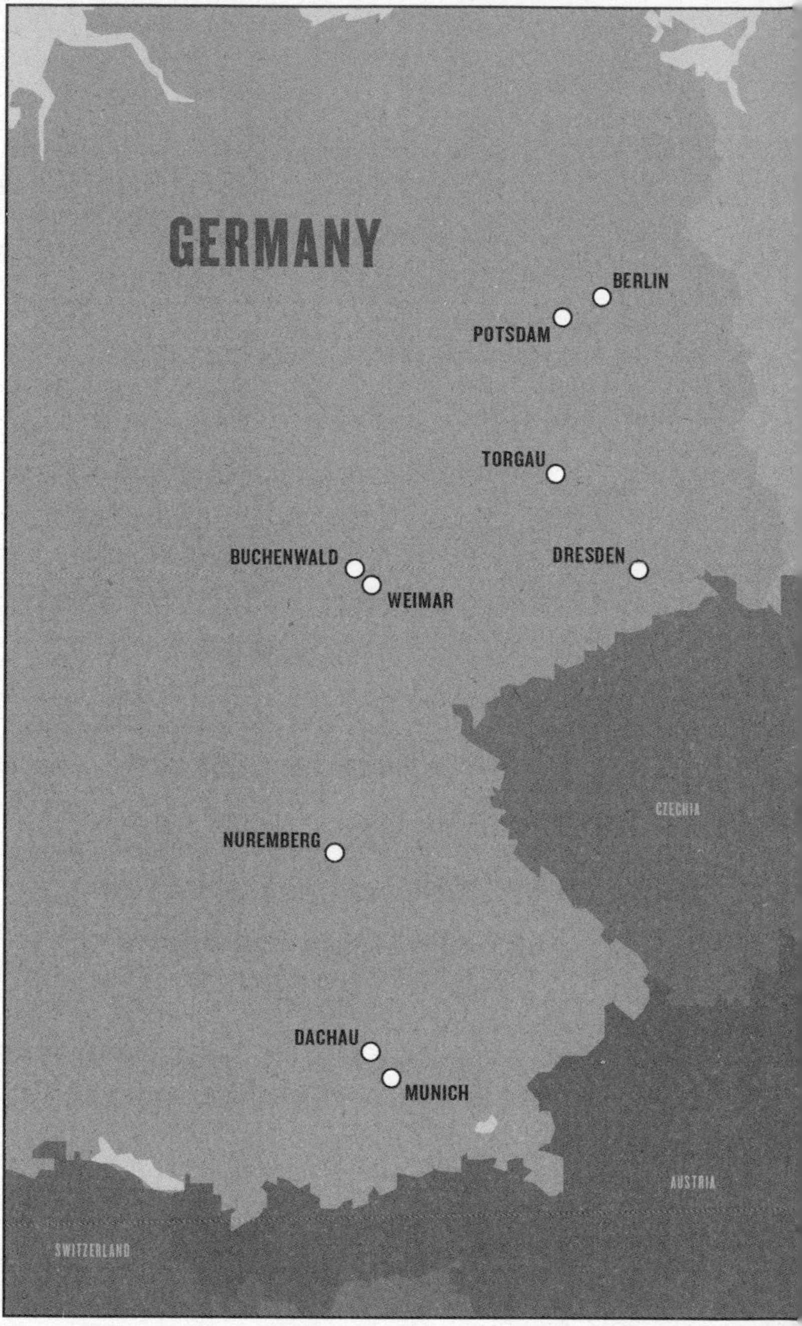

GERMANY
BERLIN
POTSDAM
TORGAU
BUCHENWALD
WEIMAR
DRESDEN
CZECHIA
NUREMBERG
DACHAU
MUNICH
AUSTRIA
SWITZERLAND

POLAND

WARSAW

WROCŁAW

BIRKENAU          KRAKÓW

AUSCHWITZ

SLOVAKIA

HUNGARY

# INTRODUCTION
## *BUS PLUNGE*

🚌 🚌 🚌

NAKED DEATH CAMP TAG.

Who knew that was a thing?

I didn't, until the breakthrough morning I opened my computer to find a must-see attachment in my Google Holocaust alert. The video shows a group of Polish citizens playing tag. Naked. In a death camp gas chamber. Again.

The whole thing is from an exhibition at Kraków's Museum of Contemporary Art, called *Auschwitz*. The title feels a little on the nose, but maybe in Polish it sounds a bit more festive. What do I know?

Try to picture it—you'll have to, the video's been taken down: a dozen sets of pasty Polish asses, flapping testicles, and breasts in full-on whitepeople frolic. Cutting loose in the Zyklon B room of the Stutthof camp in Poland, where I believe it was actually filmed, with the full cooperation of the Polish government.

It's shocking. Or was, when I started this book, back in the happy naivete of autumn 2016, when "shocking" was not yet as overused as "unprecedented."

Today, as I complete this book, in the plague year of 2021, a time of Holocaust cosplay and *Camp Auschwitz*

T-shirts, it's hard not to look back on 2016 as a time of almost poignant innocence. Five years on, we've progressed to TikTok teens rocking fake burn scars and death camp threads, lip-synching Bruno Mars, and posing as Holocaust victims in heaven. Trauma porn. While "Nazi accelerationists" gush about coronavirus as a gift to the Atomwaffen Division, the neo-Nazi fun club itching to capitalize on societal collapse to make genocide great again, an opportunity to jump-start Final Solution Redux.

By now the bar for "unthinkable" has been raised so high that not much can slime its way over. ("Very fine people" feels almost quaint.) Had the Polish government invited Trump, and let the videographer gas actual Jews, we would have been treated to the sight of the ex-president himself gallivanting along with the locals, prancing front-ass and scrotum-free among the smoking corpses. Which, if it didn't dip the needle into shock territory, might have at least provided an evening's japery for a Mar-a-Lago theme party.

Or not. My beef with Trump is far more personal, far more petty than the whole destroying-democracy and damning-future-generations thing. I blame the man for fucking up this book. Thanks to the white nationalist president, my long-ago Donald v. Adolf hot takes feel as dated as distressed denim and LL Cool J. A big chunk of book rendered hokey by contempo history.

On the plus side, it's all gravy if you're reading this while still walking upright, not felled by nuke fumes or clawing your ventilator in some tainted, eternal, COVID 19–induced solitude.

The idea, then:

Why stay in this country, listening to mere Proud Boy–esque neo-Nazis, when you could go to the source, to Poland and Germany, and experience the birthplace of actual Nazi-Nazis? How better to soak up fascist antibodies?

The concept was to chronicle a sojourn through Poland, East Germany, and World War II—essentially a two-week holiday in key hellholes and hotspots of thirties and forties Europe, as assembled by the pros at Globule Tours. "Throughout this tour," the promotional literature informs perspective clients, "you'll visit some of the concentration camps used during World War II. You'll visit the most infamous, Auschwitz and Birkenau, where you'll see chilling reminders of the Holocaust."

It's hard not to hear the whole spiel in the voice of Don LaFontaine, the Coming Attractions guy. *You'll thrill to the sight of actual ovens!*

And yes, I would be holocausting by bus.

A mode of travel, I'm ashamed to admit, as personally forbidding, for this rider, as the actual destinations to which we'll be traveling. (Lame as it is to lament one's own personal torments in the face of, say, wholesale racial purity–driven genocide, this won't stop your author from doing so anyway. With the caveat: all my problems mean nothing. And by "my" I mean yours, mine, anybody's. More or less. You want perspective, visit a crematorium in Poland.)

That out of the way, let me continue my prepubescent history of being pantsed, molested, Dirty Sanchezed, and, on one memorable, traumatic morning, actually barfed-in-mouth upon on a moving school bus.

I suffer not from motion sickness, but bus sickness.

This, plus the fact that I'm not a joiner, explains why, before ever arriving in old Europe, my testicles ascended to my lungs at the mere thought of a group-tour situation.

Beyond concentration camps—abstract, on some level, until you get there—the real hell I feared was being trapped in a rolling tour group. If Sartre was right that hell is other people—then other people in a tour bus traveling through Poland may be whatever they call the place below hell . . . or at least one corner of it.

All of which begs the question, what kind of man takes a concentration camp getaway? How fucked up would your life have to be for this to be just the pick-me-up you need to put the spring back in your step? Well, listen . . .

Let's just say, at the ass end of middle age, I found myself a little, oh I don't know, down. Disillusioned. Nothing dramatic. Unless late-night excursions to the odd extension bridge at four in the morning to stand and stare over the rail is dramatic. Some families have elongated earlobes; mine sprout suicides. My own father pulled into the garage and left the motor running at forty-nine. (Fun fact: thanks to unleaded gas, legions of desperate souls continue to try to go the carbon mono route, only to wake up with poison headaches and muffler-mouth as they stumble out of the garage and back into the kitchen for a cup of Damn-it-I'm-Still-Alive joe.)

True despair, however, would be finally getting the gumption to leap from one of those bridges, then discovering, three seconds later, the city had installed nets. As they'd done at my local leap-site. You won't just live, you'll have to hang there, like the world's biggest baby, in fishnet swaddling, until the paramedics yank you back up to continue your life of Big League Public Shame, *story at 11*. (Don't ask me how I know. Let's just say, the chafe's a bitch.)

Suicide seems to have lost its luster since the noble scene in *Godfather 2* where Tom lights Frank Pentange-li's cigar and Frank talks about ancient Rome, the glory of bathtub wrist-slitting. Google "how to hang yourself" right now and you might find, beside the Bourdain pae-ans, below the auto-asphyxiation tips, a vertical column of Euro choke-porn photos so specific in their import and ti-tles I found myself wanting to live, if only to find out who wrote the caption "Romanian Yes Lady" over what looks like a colorized snapshot of *I Love Lucy*–era Vivian Vance in hot pants, wielding a noose like a cowpoke's lariat.

And yes, if I may drop a celebrity suicide, the late An-thony B. once tossed my name out in a Q&A to be the guy to pen a tell-all upon his demise ("By the Book," *New York Times*, November 22, 2017). A suggestion I firmly believe was one more example of dark humor from a man so dark his own fans might not have realized who they were dealing with. The one time we ever discussed, you know, *jokes,* Bourdain maintained that the best ones, "as Lenny knew," don't just make you laugh, they make you squirm. Thus, after contacting me, on the first anniver-sary of his demise, about writing some "long-form non-fiction" based on Anthony's recommendation, the editor from Amazon was so horrified when I suggested the late icon would probably want hints on avoiding rope burn thrown in with Culinary Wit'n'Wisdom, said editor wrote back and told me the Amazonians had withdrawn their offer. And would I, unless I'm misinterpreting, please lose his number? Which, I like to think, made Big T chuckle in whatever high-cholesterol afterlife he now inhabits.

Recounting things now, it all seems so cornball. Collapsed marriage, fucked-up career, questionable health (mental and physical, thanks for asking). Why march out the cringey details? (There's plenty of time!) Just mush it all into a big ball of fuckups: self-sabotage, chaos, garden variety erstwhile junkie personal and professional dickishness. Add your own ingredients. "Self-hate," as Oscar Levant said, "is just narcissism with its pants on backward." (Okay, I'm lying, he never said that. I made him say it in a soon-to-be-never-made movie I wrote about the man. In its last incarnation—is that a name crashing to the floor?—Natasha Lyonne was slated to direct; *Levant* being one of the countless fun-to-contemplate, cool projects that circle the toilet for a decade or two before finally disappearing with a whoosh . . . Show business!)

Not to complain. "Self-pity," as Oscar Levant also never said, "is just—"

Never mind . . . Most people reading this won't know who Levant was anyway. That's another thing about not dying young: fewer and fewer people get your references. (I once married a smart, talented young woman who had never heard of Groucho Marx. Not her fault! I blame the Department of Education.) For the record, Levant was the first celebrity to discuss neurosis and drug addiction (his own) on TV. He was a vicious wit, concert pianist, some-time actor, and full-time Dilaudid aficionado. In the late fifties, he hosted an LA talk show whose fans used to watch to see if he'd collapse that day. My kind of guy. (Levant did say, on an early *Tonight Show*, "I get plenty of exercise. Once a week I stumble and fall into a coma." Along with "I knew Doris Day before she was a virgin." What a great Jew!) At sixty and change in 2016, I was embarrassed to still be alive. Nothing blows your credibility, in the semi-celeb ex–dope fiend business, like not dying young. Brag, brag, brag.

Twenty years ago I wrote a book about drug addiction. My own. A book that became a movie. (Insomniacs can still find it, at three a.m., on your finer cable stations.) After the book and the movie I was flooded with letters from people seeking advice or sharing their experience, or simply screaming into the void that was my AOL e-mail address.

I did not realize at the time that the real subject of that book was one I didn't even mention, the one underneath all the spoon-and-needle action. The subject of depression. It plagued me then. Plagues me now. (On the other hand, I may be straight-up mental, like my long-gone electro-shocked mother, who expired in a rest home, alone, yelling that Eichmann stole her slippers.)

Either way. Let's just say, in order to deal with all of it, I had this idea . . .

Okay then.

A minute's worth of unasked-for backstory. For entire decades before this trip, I lived with doctors barking at me that I'd be dead in a year, thanks to needle-induced hep C. Which I won't lie, I kind of enjoyed. They all said I had to do interferon, a nasty, injectable cure—some 50 percent effective—so mood-ruinous it drove two burly ex-dopers I knew to eat their guns, and one woman to drive off Mulholland Drive, only to land perfectly on a daytime soap producer's deck, then have to crawl out and pay for her own towing.

Ironically, not doing interferon is what saved my life. It qualified me for a trial drug test at Cedars-Sinai, where researchers wanted "interferon naive" patients. I am, for the record, in no way comparing myself to Dr. Mengele's twins and innocents. They come later. Plus, I was paid six hundred dollars, for twelve weeks, and only met a doctor once. The rest of the time I was ministered to by long-suffering nurses and phlebotomists, who, while gracious as pie, could not always hide their displeasure at struggling to draw blood from the sequoia-stiff veins of former IV professionals like myself. Cedars sits near Beverly Hills, so the waiting room looked like a methadone clinic with golf mags.

Sadly, the drug my team promoted—go Abbott Laboratories!—was ultimately not selected. Due, if I had to guess, to the fact that, unlike the FDA winner, HARVONI (now going for around a thousand dollars a dose, thirty in Canada), Abbott's entry packed the same mind-ripping side effects as bad acid. Some days, after my blood draw, I'd drive home hunched at the wheel, trying to steer around leering utility poles, to regrasp the concept that asphalt was solid. *The freeway is not melting* became my mantra. And I haven't even mentioned the pop-up rashes. Out-of-nowhere itching so savage it was all I could do not to yank strangers out of their cars and pay them to flay me with cheese graters. One random three a.m., unable to fight it, I actually pulled over, staggered out of my car, eased down my pants, and began rubbing my back and ass against a tree, like a bear, beside the Southwest

Museum. Inhibition banished, I crouched there shimmy-ing against the bark, yelling *Ahhhh!* like a man in a frying pan doused with gelato.

So deep was my need, I forgot how much the LAPD loved posting black-and-whites on that corner of LA, by way of catching careless speedsters running the stop sign. That night, I had the fun task of not just taking a sobri-ety test, but having the cop, a buff, bullnecked crew-cut of twenty-nine or so, search my pockets—while my pants were still at my ankles. A phenom I can still neither ex-plain nor make anyone believe. (Plus, thanks to that non-stop bloodwork, I had fresh tracks.)

"Am I going to find anything that will prick me?" the officer asked, squatting to reach into the depths of my soiled jeans. Given the strychnine and LSD brain-burn of the whole experience, I wasn't sure if he was being thor-ough or reenacting scenes from a Joe Orton play.

The upside to hep C, for me: even the most mundane day was defined by a French Foreign Legion–like defiance at the thought I'd ignored the medical experts. I was living life on the viral edge. Pre-cure, every jaunt to the 7-Eleven was like spitting in the eye of death. Post, not so much. Of course, thanks to COVID, now we could all walk around with disease-fueled paranoia. An airborne virus is easy to contract, unlike the cumbersome blood-on-blood exchange required to infect friends and family with hepatitis C.

Getting de-hepafied, in retrospect, was one of the most depressing things that ever happened to me. Sure, I was grateful, but man . . . Not dying unleashed a soul-deep sourceless despair. Maybe I hadn't achieved much in life, but damn it, I'd thumbed my nose at Western medicine, ignored advice for the twenty or thirty years the experts told me I had a year to live. I'd done something they said would kill me by default—and it didn't involve a speedball and 18th Street bangers slinging black tar balloons out of their mouths on the corner of Crack and Eightball.

So, shortly before going bussing, when a last, post-cure MRI found my liver was fine but a "suspicious mass" had sprouted on a kidney, I was weirdly elated to undress for the ultrasound. The day before leaving, the results were in. But I did not call to get them. Not because I was afraid I was doomed. Because I was afraid I wasn't.

I embarked for the Old Country with the knowledge that, thanks to the new gift pack on my kidney, I might be staring down the barrel. Again. But forget all that. The true, more mortifying truth, I knew there was no logical reason for the bone-deep sadness. My own litany of missteps and consequences was just so . . . ordinary. I was an old fuck with a young wife, two beautiful daughters (twenty-three years apart), the marriage going south, and a lifetime of regrets to relive and savor. (About which more later.) As my late Grandma Essie used to say, "Stop whining—there are people walking around with no legs!"

At least, face-to-face with the Giant Maw of Hell that was Eastern Europe in WW2, a guy would have something to justify that soul-deep desolation. For better or worse, antidepressants never worked. So instead of trying to banish the bad feeling—why not feed it? Give it a reason to live.

In the same way, when I was sixteen, and my father checked himself out, I'd been secretly relieved—handed a rational reason to feel as miserable as I'd already, irrationally, felt my entire life. Via my group tour, I hoped I could once more find relief in a situation where feeling miserable was appropriate. I could explore the land of genocide, visit sites of unspeakable suffering where bone-deep despair and depression—perhaps mankind's darkest preexisting condition—was what you were supposed to experience.

The whole plan sounds demented, now that I hear myself confess it.

But trust me, that's not even the demento part.

And yes, it must be acknowledged, given the hellish reality endured by 90 percent of the planet, my problems were luxuries. But they were still my problems. And very odd, very specific ones.

More backstory: In September 2016, when I left for Warsaw, I was, as mentioned, a married-three-times post-fifty father of a twenty-seven-year-old. I was, as well, soon to be divorced from a thirty-three-year-old (wife number three), mother of my second daughter, a four-year-old, the pair of whom—young mom and child—would, by the time I returned from the Old Country, no longer be living with me. They would be living in Texas. With Mom's mother. She was also taking the dogs.

That's right. One day you just wake up and your life's a country-western song.

But back to the backstory. (Trust me, it all ties in.)

The first time I fucked up a marriage, leaving my wife and much-adored two-year-old girl, it was because of heroin. The last time (which made the first look noble), it was for being an adulterous, self-hating, narcissistic depresso. The great thing about being a junkie: you can blame whatever assholery and devastation you wreak—generally upon the undeserving—on drugs. Take away the drugs, and it's all you, buddy. (It still pains me to remember, when the mother of my younger daughter—then three—and l decided it was over, in the first quiet after all the screams and recriminations, witnessing my ex just shake her head and sigh, "You jerk, it wasn't the cheating—it's your fucking moodiness, the depression. I don't want to raise a child around somebody so depressed.")

There, she said it.

None of the above would matter but for the stubborn fact that this story—an older guy marrying a younger woman; fathering a very, very young baby at a very, very not-so-young age, with all the mortifying and/or funny complications—was the subject of *OG Dad*, a book I went on my pal Maron's podcast to pimp. Whereupon some exec-types at ABC, listening in and sniffing surefire series material, decided to snap it up. To, as they say (apparently), "take it off the table." And give me money to turn it into some fun TV. After the whole thing, relationship and family had already imploded horribly.

How to describe this? Well, imagine you're a pilot, hired to write about the delights of flying at the very moment your plane is plunging earthward, in full nose-dive, trailing smoke. When you signed on the dotted line you were airborne. But now, basically, you're committed to rhapsodizing about the joys of air travel—making it fun!—from a smoldering crash site. A crash caused entirely by your own miscreant behavior.

I had six weeks to get the show going, to come up with a treatment one of the network execs—a willowy, sensitive, ginger fellow—found palatable. (The "treatment," for those five of you who've successfully dodged the herpes virus of show business, is a document you're required to write, describing what you're going to write, so you can get permission to write it, by the gatekeepers whose job, in Hollywood, is paying you to write. Or not write, as the case may be.)

After a month, floundering mightily, I had two more weeks to come up with something. Which just happened to coincide with the two weeks I'd be visiting concentration camps.

Meaning, to recap, at the same time I was gallivanting from Auschwitz to Dachau, I'd now be scrambling to shape a TV series around my fun-filled May–December marriage—now a flaming husk of its own—about being that frolicsome Old Guy Dad (though my child now lived in a different state), based on a book the network had snapped up—and never read. Because reading is so . . . not a podcast.

You get the setup. When Sensitive Exec finally did crack the book, opening randomly to a passage where I confess that my reasons for hooking up with a woman half my age were not entirely romantic, that part of me, paranoid of faculty-diminishing senior-hood, wanted someone who could wipe the drool off my chin in my predementia years, he was less than thrilled. It would not be exaggerating to say he was panicked. This was, after all, his career too.

And so, if the reality of my own behavior, and its consequences, was not depressing enough, I now—in the name of family entertainment—had to write as if they never happened. As if everything was still aces. For the alimony money. But hey, look at the big picture!

For Jews, lucky us, there's always reason to rant and moan, if you want to go that way. The gruesome stew of history is forever simmering.

And so, I craved the in-your-face, vicious evidence of evil. A quaint sentiment, I realize, but this was, not to wax nostalgic, before the fascist game-show-meister transformed racism, misogyny, and nationalistic violence into America's growth industries, and the entire country began buckling from Abusive Father Syndrome.

I needed something more than my own shame spiral—and its showbiz spinoff—to fortify the sadness and rage gnawing my guts. I needed to walk where Himmler walked.

I needed to go to Naziland.

# CHAPTER 1
## THE KRAMAH! THE KRAMAH!

🚌 🚌 🚌

SO I'M SHAMBLING OUT OF A CREMATORIUM during a tour of Auschwitz when suddenly these young Asian women in matching Bowie tees come running toward me squealing, *"The Kramah! The Kramah!"* I can't place the accent, but after a second I realize they're saying "Kramer," and they think I'm the actor Michael Richards from *Seinfeld*. My first thought is, *No one should squeal in a concentration camp.* My second: *How creepy is it that I look like Michael Richards?*

Of course, I feel like an egregious shitbag thinking any of this. *Here.* But that's the point. I have just stumbled from one of the stained, airless chambers in which, seventy years ago, a million men, women, and children spent their last twenty minutes naked, foaming from the mouth in screaming agony, as prussic acid scalded their lungs until they asphyxiated. The corpses, I've learned, formed a pyramid. Victims struggled for the last inch of air beneath the ceiling. Parents tried to lift their children as high as they could. The top layer was always babies.

Before the Kramer thing, waiting in line for death camp tickets, the back of my neck got sunburned. The sun was blazing and the line snaked from the death camp entrance all the way through an adjoining plaza and out to the far corner of the parking lot. But who brings sunblock to Warsaw? In September?

When I catch myself whining about being burned at Auschwitz, I want to rip my brain out, soak it in lye, and roll it in broken glass. After the gas chamber, this feels like the right response to just being part of the human race.

What is the etiquette for fending off death camp celebrity selfie requests—when, just to spice things up, you're not the celebrity?

I let the young women take a few selfies with me just to get rid of them. They want me to smile. And I glance nervously at the rest of my tour group, hoping none of them are witnessing this mortifying episode. Needless to say, it won't be the last, as we roll along through the Reichland, from camp to camp, sampling a polka party, an "authentic bratwurst dinner," and other festivities I'll be describing in the pages to come. Or trying to. Trying, because in a rare fit of domestic responsibility, I hired a cleaning person—actually, a neighbor's grandmother—to come in and tackle the nest of squalor my house morphed into after I got back and unpacked.

The thing is, no matter what I'm writing, I always start with a stack of spanking new overpriced Moleskine notebooks. And end with a pile of scribbled-on napkins, hotel stationery, ripped-out magazine pages, ad circulars, felt-tip-on-toilet-paper, or soggy coasters . . . whatever smudged, garbage-adjacent material makes it most difficult to decipher later. Picture a rottweiler-sized mound of notes, cluttering every available surface of my already book- and paper-cluttered house. A rottweiler that went missing days after my return. For the simple reason that— you're way ahead of me—said sweet, grandmotherly cleaning person thought it was trash and threw it out.

Happily, addicts—whether current or former—are great with catastrophe. So I could handle the whole suddenly solitary, formerly-noisy-now-dead-quiet house; the whole third-marriage-bites-the-dust thing. I missed my four-year-old daughter to the point of pillow-chewing. But I'm a pro, I don't register emotions, I just stuff them and drive into utility poles. But losing notes . . . *Jesus!*

After clawing my way through three garbage cans, a clogged gutter, and the fecal-caked rim of a hillside septic tank, I sat down, bit the bullet, and tried to write down every detail I could. "Every act of memory," to mangle a line from the late, great Oliver Sacks, "is to some degree an act of imagination." Or, to paraphrase Picasso, "Art is the lie that reveals the truth." Either way . . . you get the idea.

Now where were we? Right! I landed in Warsaw, dumped my bags, and, per instructions, glided into the lobby of the swanky Warsaw Hilton at six sharp to meet my fellow travelers.

I will admit that I judged everyone immediately upon stepping out of the chrome-shiny elevator. The four hearty, open-faced gentlemen lurking by the front desk are surely 4-H Club alumni, I think to myself. Solid Midwesterners who, if they have not recently milked cows, look like they'd know how.

As I step over to join the 4-H crew, two Amazonian young Polish ladies strut through the lobby, legs up to their cheekbones in see-through fuck-me heels and silver micro-skirts, escorted by a no-neck bodyguard type in wraparound shades. The women seem to have shimmied out of an old Robert Palmer video, so slinky I imagine them living on ground-up disco balls and cocaine. The muscle keeps one hand slipped inside the lapel of his jacket, either holding a gun or scratching a mole. I see the look his full-lipped companions shoot our way and die a little. I can hear their thoughts. *Och, spójrz na amerykańskich rolników!* Oh, look at the American farmers!

That night, we venture out to have dinner in some kind of kielbasa grotto. It looks like a tarted-up potato cellar, with pictures of various Polish meats lining the walls. The lighting is early bathysphere. During the meal my fellow riders and I are instructed to go around the table and say a bit about ourselves.

To one side of me sit two retired school teachers from Omaha, best friends Pam and Trudy. "Our husbands don't like to travel," Trudy tells me. "Thank God," Pam mutters out of the side of her mouth, a manner of speaking so film noir I find it instantly endearing. She's got a Lucille Ball permanent wave, permanently pursed lips, and, magnified behind unironic butterfly glasses, a no-nonsense glare I can only imagine scared generations of Omaha teens into shutting the fuck up in homeroom. Her friend Trudy's glasses hang on a rhinestone chain resting on the perpetually buttoned top button of one of those long cardigans my mother, in far-off 1960s Pittsburgh, used to call her "duster." Both opt for the same shade of blue rinse as Mrs. Slocombe in the old Brit sitcom *Are You Being Served?*, the very tint Wendy O. Williams rocked in her foot-high mohawked Plasmatics days. Right away, I liked these two, even as I felt that I'd better mind my Ps and Qs around them.

Beside the Omaha ladies is a sixty-ish bullet-headed "precision bulldozer operator" and ex–rugby player from Sydney, Dozer Bob, whose reason for the Eastern Europe tour is straightforward. "Just wanted to travel, didn't I?"

Later, after six vodkas (him, not me), Bulldozer Bob corners me to confide the sad climax to his very sad marriage—and the real motive for his trip. "My wife. She never wanted us to have company, did she? She never wanted to see anybody. I don't think we had company more than once. So I was alone, forever-like, and I thought it was supposed to be that way. Until last year, I came home from a job out of town and she was gone. The note she left? It said, 'I want to be around people.' Can you believe it?"

Oh man! It's such a brutal story, all I can do is sympathize, and steer him in a different conversational direction. I mean, I've just met the guy. Bob lights up when asked to describe the razor-thin, right-next-to-the-cliff intricacies of his dozer work. His specialty is dangerous mountaintop construction projects. "One wrong move and it's over the side, isn't it? You're talking 100,000 pounds of Caterpillar D9—with a ripper attachment—right up your arse."

As a fellow mobile-coach insomniac, Bob and I bonded. I don't know if you've had the experience of meeting someone who, for whatever reason, seems to have been saving up their most personal issues, their deepest and darkest, just for you. But I was happy to listen. Perhaps because I was an outsider, the designated weirdo, he felt he could tell me anything. (Is it in *The Decameron*, where Boccaccio says, "You can always trust a leper"?)

Facing me, on the other side of the table, is a lovely, well-coiffed, expensively tailored Japanese lady, Mariko, who informs us she works at a law office. But not just any law firm. She works in the office of the Third Circuit Court of Appeals. The federal bench. She sees the twitch grip my face when she says this but, understandably, misinterprets it as some kind of—what?—fanboy reaction to the judiciary? As in, "Oh wow, the Third Circuit. That's Delaware, Pennsylvania, the Virgin Islands, and New Jersey!"

In fact, I've got a whole other reason for freaking. My father—what are the odds?—served on the Third Circuit. Briefly. From the time he was sworn in on October 10, 1968, until February 21, 1970, the day he stopped serving. Anywhere. Because he went into our garage (as mentioned) and left the motor running. I mean, it was such a shock—not him killing himself (I'm over that), I mean her working there, in the Third Circuit. It was such a surprise that I went into blurt mode. Saying something, more or less, like, "Hey, that's crazy, my father was a judge on that circuit."

"What was his name?"

"David Stahl."

Which elicited an even more unexpected reaction: "You must be mistaken."

Mariko, clearly, did not want people taking Circuit credit when Circuit credit was not due.

"I don't," she continues tartly, "remember him. And I remember the names of all the judges. Their pictures are on the walls."

Here, two thoughts grip me at the same time. One, they took the old man's picture off the wall. Well *that's* weird and embarrassing. And two, of course I now had to explain that, well, actually, he did serve, but, you know, she might not remember his name because he didn't, like, serve very long . . .

"In fact"—here I catch myself counting on my fingers—"about fifteen months altogether, from late '68 to early '70, before he, you know . . ."

My voice trails off, leaving Mariko hanging expectantly, skeptically on my next words. Before he *what?* I could hear her thinking. Got an operation to become a woman and moved to Malaysia? Fell down an elevator shaft? Slipped on a creamsicle in front of a streetcar and expired in three evenly divided pieces? The moment stretched. And—has this ever happened to you?—I found myself wanting to say nothing, possibly never open my mouth again, and at the same time blurting, but quietly, "Well uh, actually, he kind of killed himself."

Which I instantly regret. Because really, what better info to share with someone you've never met before in your life, but you're going to be spending fourteen days with, than announcing a parent's suicide? When you were sixteen. Quel icebreaker!

The whole exchange was relatively low decibel (for once) so no one else heard, and Mariko's partner, a tall, steely-eyed athletic fellow in a windbreaker, maybe fifty, could go on and introduce himself as if nothing had even happened.

Steely Eyes announces that his name is Don, and he's a vacationing state policeman. But I already knew that.

Well, my sphincter knew it. I feel the clench before the message makes it to my brain.

It may have been a quarter century since I last had occasion to lower myself in the back of a law enforcement vehicle. But I might as well be smuggling grenades-and-crack in my pants for the guilt and cop-sweat suddenly oozing out of my pores. An ooze—and I have no proof for this—I am sure Don the Statie can sense despite the strong kielbasa waft flooding the premises. Bad enough I'd announced myself as Gerald Von Suicide, now I was squirming like a perp in a lineup.

Tad and Madge are the next couple over. T and M sport what I'd call the never-too-old-to-have-fun-at-Disney-World look. Tad: red shorts, old tennies, bald with a mullet spilling out of a backward Astros cap. Madge favors matching red shorts and a *Don't Mess with Texas* T-shirt. Tad refers to himself as a jokester. "Why Nazis?" he asks, turning to Madge to answer his own question. "I guess it's their old world charm? Kidding!"

Tad has Madge in stitches, and he cracks up my new friends the Omaha teachers too. Despite Trudy's, to me, forbidding visage, she turns out to be a total sweetheart, with the kind of laugh that makes her cover her mouth, as if surprised whenever she hears herself.

Lest I forget, that first night in the sausage grotto, my bona fides as nutritional nut-job were premiered for all my new friends. I've been a veggie for decades—function of all those "you'll be dead in a year" speeches by straight-shooting liver specialists. I may have geezed Mexican tar smuggled north in the anal cavities of enterprising drug mules, but God forbid I'd gnaw a nonorganic celery stick. And I was too superstitious to change diets. Long after I'd kicked dope and cured hep C, I still stayed away from meat. But what was in front of me here was not just meat, it was kielbasa. Growing up in far-off Pittsburgh, kielbasa was everywhere. To me, it always tasted like somebody's grandmother. But now, in this dim, low-ceilinged cave, I gulped back bile as a stone-faced waiter delivered varieties I'd never heard of. Arrayed before us, in no particular order, were: Kielbasa Krakówska—hot-smoked with pepper and garlic. Kielbasa wiejska—a U-shaped tube of pork and veal. Kielbasa weselna: wedding sausage. (Insert joke here.) And Kielbasa Biala, a white bulbous sausage, like something you'd find on a coroner's table after a fatal, Bobbitt-inspired sex crime. The full-on Castrato Platter!

Fighting off images of George Bush Senior gone green and vomiting in an envoy's lap on a state visit to Japan (anybody else remember?), I was eager to not call attention to myself. So I slurped up my żurek (sour rye soup) and made busy work of pushing sauerkraut and bigos, Poland's national bean dish, around on my plate—each of which, by the way, was emblazoned with Poland's national bird, a white-tailed eagle against a shield of red, and seemed to weigh a ton. The plates were so heavy I had to resist the urge to simply pick one up and knock myself out with it. Instead, by way of nutritional subterfuge, I found if I could cover the national bird's beak and eyeballs with chunks of national meat, I could perform something that looked like eating, until the waiter came by to clear everything away.

If I was going to make it through the meal—let alone

Poland—I knew I had to man up. I nibbled cabbage, fighting the rising panic at what I've signed on for; when I raised my eyes, I saw our tour guide, Suzannah, directly across the table from me. She's been working her way from diner to diner.

"All right there?"

"Aces," I say, hearing the word and wondering where the hell it came from.

"Aces, is it?"

Suzannah's got that certain timbre of British accent that makes you question your own intelligence. She stares for a second, and I can all but see the thought balloon over her head: *Are you going to be a problem?*

Tall, silver-haired, wire-thin, with no-nonsense black spectacles, Suzannah owns the sort of Helen Mirren at fifty-ish features that seem to modulate between fierce and pleasant. Fiercely pleasant being perhaps the perfect combo for a professional tour guide: the rolling embodiment of Carry On. The job itself, it becomes clear as we merrily roll along, exists as a blend of shepherd and *tummler*.

"Did you know," Suzannah asks, aiming an amused smile my way, "the word kielbasa is actually derived from the Hebrew, kol basar, meaning 'all kinds of meat'?"

"I did not," I say, though my first thought, of course, is why is she telling me about Hebrew stuff? Did "Honk If You Love Semites" appear on my forehead when I hit Polish soil?

Once Hebe-anoia rears its ugly head, there's no putting it back in the phylactery.

"I don't know much," I stammer, "about kielbasa history."

"And you're a vegetarian? For moral reasons?"

Not for the last time, I can't tell if our guide is needling me or making an effort to help me "feel a part of."

"Nothing moral about it," I say, wishing I hadn't. "I mean, I don't eat meat. But I'd shoot a cow just to watch it die. I just don't like the taste of hormones."

"Interesting." Now I'm getting the raised eyebrow. "Hormones?"

Way to blather! Nothing says "Aren't you glad to have *me* on this trip?" like launching into cow shooting. Seeing the expressions on my fellow diners' faces—am I imagining the hush that's come over the table?—I hear myself announce, "Hitler was a vegetarian!" And go on to describe how the führer loved his kale, pasta, and apples, and had quite the sweet tooth. "He was so terrified of being poisoned he kept a dozen adolescent girls on staff as food tasters. And flatulent? Forget about it. They called him 'der stinkbomb.' In German, I mean."

Hitler's flatulence! Adolescent girls! Talk about a great first impression. What's the Polish word for "cringe?"

Intros complete, Suzannah encourages us to go around the room and say, in a sentence or two, why we've elected to come along on the tour. I count sixteen of us. Almost everyone responds with some version of "I love the Jewish people" or "I've always been fascinated by Jews!" or "I've seen so much about the Jews on the History Channel." And, of course, the perennial "I watched *Schindler's List.*"

I'd say it's a good bet a lot of these fine folks probably haven't ever met an actual spawn of Moses. (Here I am!) And the way they say "the Jews," to me, recalls the distinctly Trumpian flavor of "the Blacks." (Remember "Look at my African American over here?") But who cares? Reflexive contempt melts away at such relentless niceness. Who the fuck am I?

By the time it's my turn, I feel like a snitch. All these normal, decent-seeming souls getting their kielbasa on in preparation for a nice, old-fashioned mass-murder tour. And me, a cynical shmohawk on board to ride along and try to capture the whole exotic spectacle. After I explain that I'm here on assignment, for a magazine, a dapper Chicago septuagenarian named Sylvan—"but call me Shlomo!"—slides his chair over and tells me he always planned to write after he retired too. Look at us! Just a couple of scribble-happy retirees!

Within minutes of meeting, Shlomo, a round-faced, beaming, fireplug of a guy, regales me with his adventures as a six-year-old in a Polish DP (displaced persons) camp before coming to America, in steerage. "I didn't get a piece of meat for three years! One time I found a salami wrapper and it was like a holiday!"

The DP centers, my new dinner pal tells me, were beyond dismal. "I was," he tosses out casually, "a brand-new orphan." Before that can sink in he barrels on: "For a while, at a camp called Babenhausen, me and the other little kids slept in what used to be stalls for Third Reich horses. We'd try and smoke the hay. The worst part was, we weren't just smelling horseshit, we were smelling Nazi horseshit.

"Another camp I got sent to was a got-damn concentration camp till a month before I got there." (Shlomo never says god-damn, he says *got*-damn. Sometimes you meet people you could listen to all day.)

I thought I knew my Holocaust, but already Shlo's telling me things I didn't know. Like how he and other "war orphans" had to live alongside real Jew haters.

"These were the schmucks who beat Jews in the street under Hitler. Supposedly they were de-Nazified, but come on! What else were they going to tell the Americans—*I still keep Hitler's picture under my pillow?* They hated us!" It's the last part—the still hating—that gets to me. His laugh is weirdly high-pitched, and contagious, but it doesn't sound happy about any of this. "Think about it, Jer." (Shlo's the one Globoid who doesn't call me Gerald.) "One day I'm running from these bastards, the next I have to shit beside them. And the food? The shit was probably tastier. Do you know what gruel is? We would have killed for gruel. Some people did. But let me tell you something, boychick, what made it okay was knowing those Nazi sons of bitches had to eat the same drek we did."

Despite the mega-grim memories, Shlomo grins big. "Oh boy," he says, taking a pause to polish off a pierogi, "we're going to be friends!" I've known him two minutes, and I love the guy.

Suzannah, I see, is conferring with Tad and Madge, our fellow travelers from Odessa. (The one in West Texas, not the Ukraine.) Their lowered voices, I'm convinced, are discussing my ridiculous veggie declaration. You want to find out how paranoid, narcissistic, and dickish you really are? Find a tour bus and hop on board. This was of course pre-corona, so the primary concerns were not viral but (in my case) psycho-emotional. One way or another, visiting the sites where your ancestors, your *people,* were slaughtered, can stir the pot.

An hour later, my pork sausage congealing on the plate, my new pal slides his seat closer. We've been sharing confidences. When Shlo tells me about his wife's colon situation—"Thank God we didn't have to get her a bag!"—I tell him about my grandpa Moishe, who got a colostomy back in the fifties, when things were really primitive. "They put this bandage on his stomach. When he had to go, he'd step into another room, peel the bandage off, pull out what looked like a little pink dog penis, and drop a deuce in a saucepan my grandmother carried around in her purse."

Silence. Was I talking loud?

Christ! I've been hanging out with sick-fuck professional ironists so long I've forgotten how to talk to non-nihilists. Shlo lets it go with a shrug. "I hope you had a good dishwasher!" And within moments we're back on track.

I must, for reasons of future bus-ride congeniality, learn some kind of verbal restraint. Not for the first time, as the trip kicks in, I make a note to myself: *Don't be an asshole*.

# CHAPTER 2
## ROADKILL

🚌 🚌 🚌

IT'S THE FIRST FULL DAY OF THE TOUR and our orders are to be up at 0600. Leave luggage in front of the door. Make it down to the meaty buffet breakfast at 0700. Be on the bus by 0800. It is, fittingly, a regimented schedule. And the whole routine—up, out, luggage by door, down to breakfast—is to be repeated daily.

For the trip, I decided to invest in a brand of luggage called Bluesmart. An outlandishly priced, hard shell, rolling bit of hardware I sprung for because it had a built-in USB port, and an app that let you Know Where Your Luggage Is. For those of you thinking of investing: don't.

Forget that using the app required night school, the USB port barely held a charge, and for all its high-tech charm, one of the multihundred-dollar snaps snapped off my second night away from home. The lock was hit or miss and—worse—the app made some kind of strange beep I was too stupid to know how to turn off when I was in the same room. It was as if my high-end suitcase, neurotic as a pure-bred whippet, was whimpering at me from across the room, *Over here! Hey! I'm over here!* I only wished I could have given it treats.

How often, really, do you need to charge your iPhone with your suitcase? I'd have been better off with a duffel bag and an extension cord. But, of course, due to the aforementioned ABC situation, the ongoing EOCM (Epic of Collapsing Marriage), and all-around techno-cluelessness, I opted to spend money I didn't have, for a device that didn't work, that I absolutely did not need. One that reminded me, with frantic beeping at random intervals, that I'd tried to suffocate it under a pile of towels behind the bathroom door. Why I thought piling towels would interfere with the nonstop no doubt GPS-connected software that let the needy device know we were ten feet from each other, is a whole other issue. And I can't blame jet lag.

(I am excising my desperate intercontinental calls to the Bluesmart help line. Though I will take this opportunity to apologize to the bevy of crack luggage technicians who bore my pleas and accusations with unceasing patience. I have no evidence, but I would venture a guess these good men and women realized, by the fifth call, this maniac with a functioning Bluesmart serial number, and a nonfunctioning brain, was less in need of suitcase solutions than psychological help. If not an outright intervention. To them, too late, I say "Dziękuję, bardzo dziękuję" and "Jestem trochę błaznem." That's Polish for "Thank you, thank you very much. I am a bit of a buffoon.")

As is my wont, once we get moving, I park myself in the back of the bus, putting plenty of seats between me and the group. My nearest neighbor, four rows up and leftward, is Patsy, the youngest member of our posse, a lavishly blond-curled Australian millennial of size who wears stunningly tight tops and refers to herself in the third person—as in "Patsy likes!" It's a linguistic touch I have always enjoyed and admired, most famously from Reggie Jackson ("That's not good for Reggie!") and oft-employed by Kanye West.

Soon enough Patsy will have a nickname. Tad from Texas will call her "Four-shot," referring to an incident of overzealous adult beverage intake that resulted (or so I heard) in some spectacular demonstration of what her Australian cohorts refer to as "technicolor yawning." No surprise, Patsy's the first to lead us in sing-alongs between sites. And, in overheard conversations, hints saucily at the "serious partying" she and her girlfriends get up to Down Under. "My girls raise hell!" she whoops. I sense no sexual component to this naughtiness. More like goofy barroom shenanigans. The lady likes her turps, as they say in Australian.

(Down the road—spoiler alert—I will walk into a plate glass door exiting the Buchenwald cafeteria, and young Patsy, though tragically hungover, will help administer paper towels to my gushing head wound. But let's not rush the fun.)

Drinking proves to be a wonderful way for my cohorts to bond. Not drinking stands out as yet another nonendearing trait, separating me from my busmates. At the end of last night's kielbasa get-together, there was a vodka toast. (Said vodka included in the prepaid meal plan.) Happy to raise my glass, I did not actually swallow. Thereby making myself a subject of curiosity and some dismay to my fellow travelers. I've heard humor is a great way of disarming uncomfortable situations. But my standard riposte (first employed during a nondrinking book tour of France—where they really treat you like a freak if you don't imbibe) fell horribly flat. "One drink"—cue desperate-to-please smile—"and I break out in handcuffs!"

The response, I recoil to even recall, was less mirth and more, oh what's the word? a sort of back-slowly-toward-the-door revulsion (especially from Don, the straight-backed statie). The truth, that boatloads of heroin left my liver the consistency of dried Play-Doh, making alcohol a bad idea, seemed like a less-than-necessary revelation. Nobody said being sober would win you popularity contests. Least of all on a Euro death camp getaway.

But back to the bus! Within minutes after parking my carcass, high school hood style, in the back, I am spotted by Suzannah, who further cements the role of hybrid top sergeant–slash–social director and invites me up front.

"Look at Gerald all by himself in the back of the bus. Well, what do you know, you've won the lottery, Gerald, and now you get to sit up front behind our wonderful driver, Josef!"

All eyes turn. Boy, is my face red! And not just because almost no one has called me Gerald since my grade school principal, Herbert W. Day, who liked to paddle little boys. (By way of revenge, Herb became briefly famous when his name was used as a pseudonym for the cowriter of X-rated 1980s art-porn epic *Café Flesh*. It's the little things.)

Josef, it should be remarked, has that Scando-Teutonic Illya Kuryakin, *Man from U.N.C.L.E.* sixties sidekick vibe. (Boomer reference alert.) There's a kindly smirk on his face. The smirk you might see on the face of a man who killed for hire in his teens, and was paid to know things about you. I like the dude. It isn't his fault I have to gulp back my buffet eggs to keep from yolk-spraying his hair. Being raised by people who hoarded saccharin packets— one visit to a Chinese restaurant and our kitchen looked like a free mustard museum—it's hard to make it through the all-you-can-eat Warsaw Hilton breakfast buffet without gorging. But the sight of bloodmeats at that time of morning puts a mild damper on the appetite. Even the toast tasted meaty.

The bus, by the way, is a beauty: white with red diagonal stripes on the sides, cleaner than my kitchen table. "A luxury motor coach," as the literature describes it. But however glamorous, a tour bus is a tour bus. (Excluding band tour buses, which, as we know from *Behind the Music*, are fun-filled, mobile dens of oral sex and glam narcotics.)

So there I am. Summoned by our leader from my last-row perch, I make the walk of shame up the aisle. Lower myself onto the Punishment Seat behind Josef the driver, with a direct view of his outpoking occiput. Suddenly, I remember a line from a John Steppling play, something like: "*My dick was hard as the back of Jesus's head.*" Steppling, I dimly recall, moved to Poland to run the National Film School. Irrelevant. Why am I jealous?

Gripped by panic, the mind seeks distraction. Because, hard as I resist, one wrong move and this entire book will sag under the weight of memories of recovered bus abuse. I have a thing about people staring at me from behind. (This may have to do with the fact that growing up in my family, you couldn't walk upstairs in front of anybody without them smacking you on the ass—or "hiney," as it was, curiously, called in das Stahl-haus.)

The point is, I like people where I can see them. But

it's more than that. It's a long story, possibly involving the words "gym teacher" and "taint." Parked school buses, in a certain Pittsburgh high school, way back when, were great places to ditch algebra. But if your luck ran out, Coach D, a massive, psychotic former third-string placekicker for the Steelers, would pry open the doors and clomp down the aisle, popping a ham-sized fist in his palm, until he found you crouching on the grimy school bus floor. And then you were lunch meat.

It's best, I think, not to declare my phobia, or its unseemly origin, to my new companions.

"The cheese stands alone," comes a voice from a few seats away, which I have come to recognize as Tad, the jokester half of Tad'n'Madge from Texas. "Looks like somebody got a bad case of the onesies," Tad cracks, with a roadhouse wink in my direction. Everybody's a comedian. He closes his eyes, mimes wrapping your arms around the one you love, and bursts into a gurgly, Hank Williams Jr.–stabbed-in-the–Adam's apple C&W tune: *Oh, I'm huggin' the pillow in Poland, chewin' pierogi alone . . . I'll be kickin' myself in Kraków, missin' my schnitzel back home . . . Wait!*—Tad's voice goes low and Redd Foxxy—"you think Jerry's got a schnitzel?"

"Let's hope so!" It's Mr. Swertz, father of twenty-something Dahlia, who are traveling and sharing a room together. (Later, Mr. Swertz, a civil engineer from Missouri—"call me Del"—confides that he and Dahlia lost Mrs. Swertz last year, and this was a trip she always wanted to make.)

Everybody's a sad comedian.

I feel like my hair is burning.

Tad holds out his hands for an air hug. "No offense, buddy."

I ignore the hug thing. "None taken, pally."

Did I just say "pally"? What am I, in *A Bronx Tale*?

I may as well be wearing a dunce cap. Plopped up front, squirming, it's like I've been shot up with elementary school NARCAN, reliving a lifetime-in-a-minute of no-seat-in-study-hall, look-at-the-funny-Jew shame as it's chemically squeezed out of my system. Being one of two Jews in a grade school of eight hundred, patterns are formed. (The first time I actually *was* shot up with NAR-CAN, in a bus station toilet, I felt less squirmy when I came to staring up at a bored-looking janitor than I do now, up here behind Josef, being scrutinized—or so I imagine—by these festive strangers.)

Madge, of Tad'n'Madge, comes to my rescue: "Don't listen to him, Gerald. Tad's drunk on his butt. And it's only five minutes before decent."

"Darlin', I'm still on Texas time," Tad kids. Then gives me another wink.

"Guess you can tell, I'm the Captain and she's Tennille."

He keeps going till Madge elbows him. Stage whispers, "Knock it off!"

"Okay, hon."

Then, sotto voce again, "Sorry, Gerald!"

Christ!

Because of the pressure—the rows of death campers staring at me from behind—I begin to sweat. A bad enough situation, complicated by the fact that, rushing out this morning, I was unable to open my high-tech app-requiring suitcase. (The gimmick, as mentioned, is you open it from your phone. As if somehow this is an improvement on Stone Age technology like an actual key. Or a combination. Which now seems insane.)

I'm plagued by a sinking fear that whatever clothes I have on my back this minute might be the same ones I'll have on my back in fourteen days, when I fly home.

At the rate my perspiration is morphing me into a two-legged shame sponge, if I don't act fast I'll squish. To-night, when we get to the Kraków Marriott, or wherever we're lodging, I'll have to see if the concierge can scare up a crowbar. If I put my back into it, I'm hoping I can pry my suitcase-of-the-future open. It's that or stick a smidge of C-4 in the USB port.

When Suzannah takes her special seat, next to the wall beside the front exit, I turn to meet her eyes. Can't she see the living hell my banishment has wrought? The woman is made of stone!

No way around it, I am going to sit for hours with a gaggle of humans behind me aiming their eyes at the nape of my neck. It's the first time, as a grown man, I've wished I had a mullet. The setup induces the same crawl-out-of-my-skin-and-slide-down-a-carrot-peeler sensation as kicking dope. Okay, not as intense; but the same genus of *squirm*.

Adding to this unease is a sensation I'd guess a lot of people suffer while piling through former Nazi turf. Peer into a café, step onto an elevator, and you can't help but wonder if every hairy-nostriled old-timer giving you stink-eye has a secret history. Case in point: the sausage-bobbling geezer at an adjoining table this morning at breakfast in Warsaw. I wondered if the old bastard was aware he was scowling at me. (I should probably explain that as I've aged, a map of the Negev seems to have blossomed over my eyebrows. It wasn't there when I was young. I'm not even sure it was there the previous year. But now there's no escaping. I've got *Natural Born Juden* stamped all over my mug.) So there's no way to tell if the old Pole's pierogi-charged piles are killing him, or if, in happier times, he was skewering Jew babies just up the road. He's got a greedy eater's face, as if, long ago, he had not just bayonetted, or gassed, infants of lesser races, he had eaten them, finger by finger, limb by limb. And was feeling nostalgic.

Like my grandfather used to say, "If you ever forget you're a Jew, a gentile will remind you." Especially, no mystery, a Third Reich gentile. It would probably help if I stopped staring.

I'm hoping this paranoia abates as I relax into the Hebe-Killing Countries. Instead, it worsens. The problem, when Nazis are involved, is that paranoia doesn't register as paranoia. It's just there. Like gravity. Seeming equally inevitable and appropriate.

# CHAPTER 3
## STALIN'S SYRINGE, LUCKY JEWS, AND A WARSAW COWBOY

🚌 🚌 🚌

SO WHERE ARE WE OFF TO, on opening day of our voyage through history? We are heading off to see Warsaw's famous "Wedding Cake" Palace of Culture and Science. Plainly, the Globule masterminds understand that you can't just dump folks into genocide-ville. You need to be fluffed a little first, see some cheerier sites.

On the way to the palace, Suzannah, from her perch by the door, tells us about the mythical Mermaid of Warsaw, who once upon a time fell in love with a local fisherman and devoted herself to protecting the city. Suzannah tells us to keep our eyes peeled for mermaid doorknobs, a small nod to the heroine from local residents. It's a sweet fable. A way to ease into the trip. We need to hear a pretty story before diving into ugly.

We also learn that Hitler pledged to "leave not one stone standing" in the City of Mermaids. And that the Marshall Plan was not extended to Poland.

Impressively, Suzannah does not work off of notes. "In 1596 the Royal Court moved from Kraków to Warsaw. You'll notice linden trees are planted along the Royal Way. Warsaw is the greenest city in Europe, with eight hundred species of flowers on display at the Festival of Flowers . . ."

When we finally arrive at the famous Wedding Cake, our leader manages to make the architectural oddity hugely interesting. "In the Stalin era, the building was known as the Joseph Stalin Palace of Culture and Science," she explains, all but holding open her arms and going all *Little children, gather 'round* . . . "After Stalin, they took his name off the front, and out of the lobby. But you don't live through Stalin without a sense of humor, and today Warsaw locals who don't refer to it as the Wedding Cake prefer 'Stalin's Syringe,' or 'Elephant in Lacy Panties.'"

Having had some experience with syringes, I get the Stalin thing. The Elephant in Lacy Panties, I suspect, may involve vodka. That said, the building does stand out as a jarring combination of phallic and fussy. But I don't get to a lot of weddings.

Stepping off the bus, I realize there is no self-esteem booster like pulling up to some prosperous corner of a thriving metropolis and stepping off a big striped bus with your Globule strap around your neck—showing colors!— while receiving marching orders from a stern tour guide. That strap, by the way, is to hold our "Whisper," a blocky, black, shaped-like-a-nineties-cell-phone wireless headset that enables the tourist-listener to hear what the woman in charge is saying without having to crowd her like baby lambs around a mama sheep. The feeling is not unlike that of being in rehab, and riding a van to a baseball game, knowing folks regard you as mentally challenged when you step off the bus in the parking lot.

Embarrassingly, once my feet hit the ground, it's all I can do not to sneak into Stalin's Syringe, dash up the stairs, and jump off the roof. Perhaps, in the Stalinist style, I'd be officially disappeared from group Globule photos, as if never having existed. (In the Red-scared sixties, when Cold War grade-schoolers practiced ducking and covering in case of a Russian A-bomb attack, more than one suspicious schoolmate wondered aloud if Stahl might be short for Stalin. (*He's not just a Jew—he's a commie!*) I decided not to leap when I remembered something an ex-coroner's assistant I met on a brief *CSI* gig told me about the souls who go that route. Without getting technical, she detailed over tuna salad how, on impact, all your organs shoot out of your rectum. Or vagina, if you have one, "We didn't call them jumpers. We called them spray cans." Science!

After the Wedding Cake we stop in a charming square, where I pop into a souvenir shop and buy some little Jews. Carved from linden trees, the popular souvenirs are about the size of salt shakers, and along with hand-painted beard and money bags, they come with an actual coin clutched in the rabbi's hand. The shelves are full of them.

I ask the storekeeper, a grinning man named Lek with a trim, pointy beard, no mustache, and a pearl-button country-western shirt, "What's the significance of the little Jews?" He is more than happy to explain.

"They're cute, ja? They are zydki. Lucky Jews. Put them by the door, so money won't go out of the house." While I chew on that, he amplifies: "In Poland we have saying, 'A Jew in the hallway—a coin in the pocket.'"

I take six. Because—why not? On the one hand, it's a racial stereotype. The rabbi's holding a coin! On the other, I could use some financial assistance, so why not give it a shot? Maybe they'll work. Compared to, say, Julius Streicher cartoons, full of big-nosed Jews with bulbous lips and dripping fangs clamped around the throats of pale *junge frau*—innocent young women—these rabbi dolls feel almost benign. All Talmudic beard and soulful eyes. But maybe benign is more insidious

Along with the figurines, I discover, paintings of Jews counting money are popular items in Polish homes. Who doesn't want a Jew counting money hanging over the sofa? For folks who, historically, hate Jewish people—to the point of helping Germans gas them—they kind of love them too. At least symbolically. Perhaps I should be more offended. Am I investing in kosher lawn jockeys here?

As if reading my thoughts, Mr. Lek adds, "Is happy stereotype. Nostalgic."

I can tell he means well. Better a hand-carved shekel-clutching rabbi than a vicious Chasid slitting a Christian baby's throat for matzoh sauce. Though I'm guessing they have those too, you just have to ask. Knock twice on the counter and he'll shlep in with a stash from the back.

Funny, or questionably funny story: a few years ago a Canadian Jew named Michael Rubenfeld, an actor, decided to film himself appearing in a Polish market on Easter Sunday dressed as the ever-popular "Jew with a coin." Mr. Rubenfeld set up a stall where he peddled objets d'art featuring his own image. Dressed as the archetypal coin-clutching Yid, the actor made a bucket of zlotys taking selfies with shoppers. The film of his adventure was presented at a Jewish alternative arts festival.

Again, the Poles traditionally are no great fans of the sons of Moses. According to *Jewish World,* as recently as

2013, 63 percent of Poland's citizens believed in a Jewish conspiracy to control banking and the media. (Who knew they had *Breitbart Poland?*) Ninety percent had never met a Jew. Twenty-three percent believed things like, "Christian blood is used in Jewish rituals." Who wants borscht?

Before I can vacate the premises, Lek opens a drawer and pulls out a box, ready to show me the next surprise. I half expect the head of a cantor. Instead, he lifts out a cowboy hat. That's right. Turns out Lek's a giant country-western fan. And he's not alone. Every year, he announces proudly, there's a country music fest in Mrągowo, not too far away, called Piknik Country. (Which explains his pearl-buttoned shirt.)

Lek's favorite is Polish cowboy star Michael Lonestar, a regular headliner at the Piknik hoedown. Just in case I'm not impressed, he holds up his phone and thrusts it across the counter to show a video of Mr. Lonestar, who resembles a beefy Johnny Winter, Johnny Winter if he'd been force-fed pierogies and chained in a Gdansk root cellar for twenty years. It's a cool look. The tape's from a live show, and Lek sings along for a couple of lines, inviting me to join in. (Why wouldn't I know the lyrics?) Listen:

> For lunch I had some exhaust fumes and drank
>   Coca-Cola
> But I've got good companions, my rifle and my horse
> Oh, you can make fun of my country music, but
>   that's okay
> I've got the bullets, and I'm staying the course . . .

Or something like that. Apologies to Mr. Lonestar if

I've got this wrong. The Polish cowboy, Lek informs me, had some of his songs banned in the eighties by the authorities, who found them politically provocative. Glancing left and right, Lek leans forward and whisper-sings some of the offending lyrics: *"There's a prairie on my screen, and Siberia outside . . .* He's like your Ernest Tubb, no?"

Well, yeah!

Perking up again, Lek lets me know that Lonestar tours with his own troupe of "country ladies." Once more he thrusts the phone at me. Now, I think, he's showing off, as we ogle a trio of denim micro-skirted young women onscreen—"They're called Sexy Texas!"—who perform some fancy, if disturbingly sluggish, dance moves behind the star.

"We love the line dancing," Lek continues plaintively. "I want so bad to go to your Branson!" Where, I'm guessing, he won't see a whole lot of little Jews, coin-clutching or otherwise.

Leaving the gift shop, I'm on the lookout for more signs of *Hee Haw*–friendly Poles, but don't see any. Residents, from my just-got-here-a-minute-ago tourist's vantage, are almost uniformly well-dressed, in Midcentury Conservative Nice-wear. Armies of button-down shirts, all ironed and tucked in, and shiny shoes. None of your nonstop T-shirt-and-jeans so prevalent here in sloppy America. (Let alone any ten-gallon hats.)

I clutch my rabbi bag when we get off at our next stop and saunter over to what's left of our second destination: the Warsaw Ghetto.

The Warsaw Ghetto, for those in the audience who

don't have grandfathers named Moishe, is where Nazis stuffed Jews—not just those from Warsaw, but rounded up from nearby towns as well. At its height there were nearly half a million humans crammed into a 1.3-sqare-mile area. Essentially, the Jews were walled into a vertical coffin. (Since this book's original publication, Russian American journalist Masha Gessen has been attacked, on the occasion of receiving the Hannah Arendt Prize—in Germany—for comparing the Gaza Strip and the Warsaw Ghetto. Which opens up the whole *Mein Kampf*-ed, blood-libel, anti-Semitic, Islamophobic, rampantly racist full-on-fascism-to-keep-us-safe-from-vermin situation. *MAGA Unleashed.* By the time you read this, the camps may already be opening. Let's all promise to write! To paraphrase Gessen, we know one thing they didn't know ninety years ago: we know that the Holocaust is possible.)

I recall, from researching a novel about Joseph Mengele (yes, I've had Nazi-osis for a while), how Third Reich nutritionists decided that, if residents consumed fewer than eight hundred calories a day, they'd all be dead in under a year. They had a lot of scientists on that. All the best people. The plan was slow-motion genocide. Mulling about the four-meter wall the authorities built to keep undesirables from escaping, it's hard not to think of a certain other world leader's passion for The Wall. If the world is divided into Undesirables and You, then you are always going to need a wall to keep them out. Or, in the case of Warsaw, in.

"One survivor," Suzannah tells us, "was Roman Polanski. Who of course went on to make *The Pianist*."

"Well, that's *one* thing he went on to do," Tad cracks. "The rascal!"

Before the war, 10 percent of the population was Jewish. Thanks to three million being murdered during World War II—90 percent of Polish Jewry—there are now only twenty thousand or so left in the country. Meaning, in effect, there are tons more wooden Jews in Poland than nonwooden Jews.

Again, I have to ask myself, was it wrong to drop a couple hundred zlotys on a dozen lucky-charm rabbis? Was I cosigning deep-seated bigotry or helping the local economy? The jury's out.

One zloty, by the way, is worth a quarter. The bill even looks shabby. It's the Burt Young of international currency. What else are you going to do with it but buy tiny Jews?

In a tragic example of the law of unintended consequences, Suzannah informs us that the failure of the Nazi plan to starve out five hundred thousand Warsaw Jews spurred the high command to grease the wheels for another, more surefire solution. The final one. Wherein they built camps and packed the future dead onto boxcars. By strange coincidence, decades before the prison-industrial complex became America's hottest growth industry, the prison business was booming in Eastern Europe. Hiring workers to add chimneys and crematoriums could be a real jobmaker! (Hard not to imagine Steve "I Financed Seinfeld" Mnuchin on *Meet the Press*: "Say what you will about the Third Reich, they were big on infrastructure!" Or, as a certain ex-president told his chief of staff during a 2018 trip to France, Hitler "did a lot of good things.")

# CHAPTER 4
## GOOGLE "POLISH BUS RASH"

🚌 🚌 🚌

BY DAY FOUR—HOW DID I LOSE THREE DAYS?—I am googling "Polish bus rash." No such malady. Which means I'm either Patient Zero or my nether-chafe is the function of excessive tour grouping. Whatever the case, I try to put the complaint out of my mind. After all, we're at a lovely polka-and-pierogi dinner outside the city and I've just discovered a hitherto—to me—unknown subculture: perma-tourists. As an outlier, I've made friends with two permas, who are also kind of outliers: a septuagenarian gay couple from San Diego, one of whom, a tiny, sardonic ex–Cadillac salesman named Douglas, leans over my plate during the polka portion of the evening and tells me he knows I'm a ringer. "You're no real tourist, buddy. We've been to dozens of these. You're not one of us."

And yes, it is hard not to flash back to the scene in *Freaks* when the drunken sideshow denizens chant at Cleopatra, the conniving trapeze artist, "Gooble gobble, one of us! Gooble gobble, one of us." At this point, however, I see no need to bring *Freaks* into the proceedings, even if I do feel like one.

The polka band, by the way, is spectacular. Eight hearty sisters of a certain age in matching "folk wear": embroidered blouses, billowing white skirts, red boots, and squares of cloth atop their heads, lying flat, like napkins dropped from on high. The sisters handle everything from clarinet to fiddle. The babushka on bass plays like Slim Jim from the old Stray Cats, if Slim Jim lived in the body of your grandmother, and your grandmother ate her grandmother. These are not dainty women. Like many middle-aged ladies I've seen in Poland, the sisters bear an alarming resemblance to Charles Bronson. (Strangely, many young men are cheekbone doubles for Melania, though unlike Bronson, who was half Polish, Mrs. Trump is straight-up Slovenian.) When they get older, from my unscientific sidewalk observation, Poles of both sexes transish to full-on Santa Klaus Kinski.

While the entertainment is sparkling, it's hard to kick back and enjoy. Beyond the fear of being yanked out of my seat and made to polka, I'm gripped by some whispering dread. For days, after all, we've been spoon-fed gruesome nuggets of Polish history. Like—this is completely random—how in 1648 a quarter of the Jews in rural southern Poland were slaughtered in a peasant revolt. Back then, one of the few professions open to Hebrews was collecting taxes and rent money for landlords, who no one wanted to pay. (As you might have guessed, it was safer to kill Jews than landlords.) Or how, in 1942, in a village outside Białystok, locals set upon their non-Christian neighbors with axes, sticks, and nail-studded clubs. Men had their eyes gouged out and babies were thrown on the ground and trampled. Nazis, looking on amused, ordered the Jews who could still walk to frog-march into the town square and sing, "*We caused the war! We caused the war!*" (I'm guessing it's catchier in the original.)

All of this, on a moonless night in a polka parlor miles outside of Warsaw proper, becomes more than history. Becomes possibility. I have a polka headache, function of flashbacks from my Pittsburgh youth, when I was force-fed Frankie Yankovic on WZUM and had to dance with my grandmother, who I loved, but, product of diet or medicine, smelled like she'd stashed rancid cabbage in her armpits. A smell I'd completely forgotten about until arriving in Poland. Maybe it is the smell of Poland. (If countries have a national smell, might ours be Success, from Donald Trump's line of male eau de toilette?) Or maybe the cabbage fumes were wafting from my own pores. I've got a lot of Polish in me.

The rustic décor features an up-to-the-ceiling shellacked tree, on which perch a trio of stuffed pheasants. I resolve, if the gówno hits the fan, to tear off a sharp branch—or pointy-toed pheasant—and swing it. Not to say there are actual Nazis lurking in the shadows. But ghosts are everywhere.

The thing is, I'm not usually paranoid. Or *this* paranoid. But I'm not usually in Poland. Douglas spots my twitchy reverie and snaps his fingers in front of my unibrow. "Anybody in there?"

"Ahhh, sorry," I mutter, scraping my brain to remember what we were talking about. Oh, right. "How," I ask, "did you know I was a ringer, Douglas?"

"Because you try and sit by yourself." He helps himself to the rest of my Polski naleśniki and continues: "That's a no-no." He and his partner, Tito, are professional tour-groupers, fresh off a thirteen-day stint in Ireland. After our concentration camp jaunt they're heading directly to a twenty-one-day Alaskan cruise. Seniors on a budget, they're both fans of how affordable trips like this are. Among regular permas, naturally, there's much chatter about the relative merits of the current tour versus epic tours past.

"Tour guides make it or break it," Tito tells me. "Suzannah's too laissez-faire. Too many choices. It's like, are we meeting at the Chopin fountain in twenty minutes or Goethe's pajamas in an hour? When we had free time this afternoon, I couldn't find the bus!"

"I told you, carry your phone!" Douglas chides, then turns to me with a long-suffering sigh. "I tell him and tell him, this is the twenty-first century. If he gets lost one more time I'm going to put a chip in his anus."

Tito waggles his eyebrows, Groucho style. "Chip who?"

Douglas is not amused. He wraps his arm around Tito's shoulders and yanks him in close. "Excuse us."

While the fun couple engage in a private confab, I strike up a conversation with Trudy, the lively ex-high school English teacher, forking pickles across from me at the table. Half shouting over a clarinet solo that could burn off ear hair, Trudy shares about her daughter's meth problems. (Again, that's the great thing about being an outsider—people confide.) "The stuff's all over Nebraska," she sighs. "In high school, all her friends had teeth like rotten cheese. Anna Lee actually poked a hole in her face. She thought there were bugs in her skin. They all do."

"That's pretty common," I say.

"Well it didn't used to be!" Here Trudy stops, shakes her head, raises her hand, and makes a circle with thumb and forefinger. "I'm talking about an actual hole the size of a quarter. One day it was just there! My little Anna Lee . . . It breaks your heart." She stops for a moment, like she forgets she's talking, before piping up again: "Have you ever heard of that?"

"Yes," I tell her, without elaborating. Maybe I do have an ex-wife who, in the grips of a savage crank addiction, claims to have picked at a cheek scab until she made a hole wide enough to stick a Marlboro through. It is not necessary, I decide, to parade this little anecdote out over stewed pork knuckles.

"It's just so awful," Trudy says, "seeing somebody you love do that to themselves."

The woman's grief is so close to the surface, it's all I can do not to start crying myself. I don't know the etiquette. Is it okay to weep publicly on a bus tour with strangers, many of whom hail from the Midwest? What if it turns into that weird kind of crying where you can't stop, and then turns into laughing. Like in *Shock Corridor*. Cry-laughing. Experienced, as a rule, on an asylum bench while the main character walks by on his first day wrongly locked in the madhouse.

I'm not even a weeper. But this is so goddamn sad.

"My little Anna Lee," Trudy says. "You have kids?"

"Two daughters, twenty-seven and four," I say. And, used to the looks this gets me, I add my usual coda: "Long story."

"I'll bet it is," she says, with less judgment than weary wonder. "You're nice to listen."

"Not at all!" I say.

Nice lady.

Thus far (not to sound melodramatic), I've tried to keep the seething cauldron of my own depression from splashing onto other riders. (Maybe "overflowing toilet" is the better metaphor.) Either way, it's easy to deflect your own shit by listening to somebody else's. And a damn nice thing to do!

You can be sincere, in a self-serving kind of way. Is that not possible?

You can be dying inside about fucking up a marriage—another one, that's half the reason you're in Poland—but your pain's meaningless. Compared to the deeper realization, the one that matters: the fact that your egregious behavior twisted the life of yet another woman who trusted you, altered another innocent child's trajectory. (Is the truth that some guys are better absentee dads than on-the-spot ones? Everybody's got their strengths.)

It takes something big to block that kind of realization. And we haven't even gotten to the professional reversals. Beyond the *OG Dad*, TV-version-of-my-life stuff. There was a life-changing, globally announced movie gig in there somewhere, writing *The Thin Man* for Johnny Depp (who, God bless him, optioned another one of my books in perpetuity; meaning, when atomic cockroaches roam the earth, we'll still be waiting for the greenlight). Until, in the midst of an awkward lunch with the director and his partner in their Malibu beachfront, I blurted, in some unfunny, apropos-of-nothing aside over salad Niçoise, "I couldn't plot my way from here to the parking lot." That's all it took.

All true. Not the can't-plot part—well, maybe—but the announcing-it-for-no-reason part. Even now, the memory makes me squirm. But I guess, I don't know, do some people, victims of childhood trauma or faulty brain wiring, maybe want to squirm? Maybe need to? Or is it me? It's like some kind of IMDB Tourette's. "Hey, I've got a jumbo screenplay deal, a gig every writer in captivity wanted, and I love the material—so why don't I just blurt something insane to instill complete fear in the people who really need to believe in me, and blow the gig?" Hilarious!

That said, the director did take time off to tape an episode of the epic Fox show *So You Think You Can Dance*. Not that there's anything wrong with that. Gosh no. Nothing. Watch me try to do the rumba. (I flunked square dancing in third grade because my partner, Janice Burkowski, was two feet taller than me, and had palms like wet sirloin.) But where was I? I'm supposed to be writing about concentration camps, and I can't concentrate.

(Am I alone here in having to battle my own destruction, at my own hands? With whatever arrows fall out of the self-sabotage quiver—narcotics, nerves, boobism, professional insanity? Is it me? What is the opposite of dress for success? What am I wearing now?)

*Irony!* I wanted to scream out there on the Malibu beachfront, when I saw the look on said director and said director's partner's face. *I was being ironic!* But too late. The pooch was screwed. I remember there were surfers out on the water. And I thought to myself, *Do they ever just drown ironically? Why would anyone do that?* Well, hey, *I* did.

A man can give up heroin, but that doesn't mean he can pry his fingers off his own throat.

Maybe if you don't have the guts for suicide, you can

kill your—pardon the expression—career, or kill your relationships, to kill the part of you that needs to kill things. *There's* a plot!

Anyway . . . after all this, I felt so cornered, so nervous about ever writing again, that I banged out a novel—actually two novels, in the same year. One for a small publishing house that paid nothing; one for an, as they say, big publisher that paid actual money but was pissed at the fact that I had (dementedly) released the other book, burning up most of my media connects to promote it before the "big one" even had a chance to drop. So, of course, said big pub decided to abandon it. As if the novel were a newborn dropped outside a fire station. (Is it maybe—just spitballing here—the case that the bigger the abandonment issues, the bigger our commitment to being abandoned? To abandoning ourselves?)

Does this make sense? Is there a future in self-help if you can't help yourself?

So what have we covered? Professional and personal land mines, self-planted and stepped on at the same time. Mentioned, forgive me for repeating, only by way of backstory—the *that* that happened before any of *this* happened.

Now let us pause for a moment to consider the ways in which divorce in contempo California differs from divorce in Nazi Germany. In California, you have to wait a year. "To cool off." Cali does not make it easy! In Hitler's Germany—compare and contrast—they did make it easy. If adultery had been committed, boom, you were both out of there. Easier still if you were an Aryan, you could just say you were misled into marrying a non-Aryan, and double-boom. Not only were vows with a racially inferior partner instantly dissolved, the non-Aryan might very easily be hauled off at three in the morning (the SS's favorite go time) and never seen again. The divorce rate soared—but so did the remarriage and subsequent birth rate. The Third Reich was all about that birthrate. Win-win, if you're a full-blooded Aryan who wants to "move on." (As opposed to a non-Aryan who got left behind.)

But enough about me. This trip was engendered in despair and (aspirationally) a cure for it at the same time.

# CHAPTER 5
## *EMPATHY PARTY*

🚌 🚌 🚌

TRUDY'S MENTION OF HER DAUGHTER'S TRAVAILS triggered a psychic firestorm of its own. But why linger? If the best cure for your own problems isn't listening to somebody else's, it's at least a beneficent distraction. Saint Francis got it right, even if he was talking to birds. The gift of empathy—or its dirty little secret—is that when you pour all your feeling into other people's pain, you don't have to feel your own. *Better to console than to be consoled.* At least theoretically.

Quickly changing the story back to Trudy, I ask how Anna Lee is now. By way of reply, Trudy pulls out a leather wallet, worn down to a patchy gray, with a somehow heartbreaking broken snap. She slides out an old-school wallet-size photo and hands it to me. Anna Lee is a dimpled twentysomething with a sweet smile. No black teeth or face divots. Just a defiant faux-hawk. All-American, down to the faintly cracked-glass glaze of her eyeballs. "She's so pretty," I say. "She's got your nose."

"You know what?" Trudy says. "She's great." She stares at the photo for a few moments in baffled joy. "I prayed so hard my husband thought I was turning nutty. But it worked! She decided she didn't like college and switched to a beauty academy, and now she's in mortician school. Like I always told her, it's all about finding something you love to do."

"A mortician has to be good with face and hair."

"Why, that's true. But how do you know that?"

It occurs to me that this may be unnerving knowledge to possess, so I explain that I once wrote a story on undertaker schools. Tell her I met a lot of really great kids. *Six Feet Under* got it wrong. They weren't creepy. (Well, not all of them.)

Perhaps sensing we've gone too deep, Trudy's friend Pam sits down and aims a conspiratorial smirk my way. "Trudy tell you we heard from the hubsters? Couple of beer drunks." Pam mimes knocking back a cold one. "On a good day," she adds, as Trudy tucks her wallet away, "it's just beer."

"Pam, for God's sake," Trudy says, but not angrily. I get the feeling these ladies have done some serious teachers' lounge time back in Omaha.

"The boys are lonely," Pam snarls, doing her side-of-the-mouth thing. "Serves 'em right, stayin' at home while us girls here sashay off." She gives me a brazen once-over. "Talking to strange men."

Just then Pam and Trudy are snatched up in a Polish conga line and, clearly thinking the same thing I am— *Please, God, don't make me two-step!*—Douglas gives me a nod and we duck out a side door before one of us gets swept onto the dance floor and gang-polkaed.

Oddly—or not—a cult of "Hitler polkas" has sprung up in the universe. It's a thing. What some people have decided to do, with their short, fun time on earth, is make stop-action videos of Hitler cut to catchy electro-polka. Whether there's more, and the Hitler polka trend is linked to the Polish government's 2018 decision—announced on January 27, Holocaust Remembrance Day—to imprison anyone who says publicly that Poland had any responsibility for the Holocaust, remains a mystery. The country's argument, essentially, is *Hitler made me do it!* Saying otherwise can get you three years in Polish jail. (Auschwitz may have been physically in Poland, staffed, you know, by Poles, but let's not jump to conclusions. It's not like, before the Nazis blitzkrieged in, it ever popped into a Pole's head to ax-murder a Jew.)

Outside the restaurant the air smells strongly of diesel, and Douglas makes a show of wrinkling his nose.

"You okay?" I ask.

"I'm fine," he insists, "I just don't like this reek." (I am reminded, suddenly, of Polish country star Michael Lonestar's line about eating exhaust for lunch. Nailed it!) "And I'll tell you what else," Douglas continues, "I do not love paying sixty-eight bucks for Polish tacos."

"That's what pierogi means in Polish," Tito chimes in, before we know he's there, "tacos. I bet you could blind taste-test with a bunch of Mexicans and Polacks, and they wouldn't know the difference."

"Whatever," Douglas says, "it's highway robbery."

No sooner do we prepare to pack up our overpriced Mex-o-Pole snacks and head back to civilization, then our tour mistress informs us of a change in plan. We'll be sharing a bus with another group. The Poles, it turns out, have a no-nonsense policy when it comes to drivers getting their proscribed rest hours. And our estimable wheelman, Josef, has been balling the jack since seven this morning. Far longer than the proscribed twelve, or maybe it was eight—the napkin I jotted the stats on is butter-and-chive-smeared—hours. So Josef had to hang it up for the day. Roaming inspectors, we learn, comb the highways for violators. (Which, side note, may be one reason you never read about Polish bus plunges.)

So it is that pro bus-tourists Douglas and Tito; the chatty high school teachers, Trudy and Pam; my pal, former displaced child Shlomo; wisenheimers Tad'n'Madge from Texas; Bob the Bulldozer; Dad and Daughter Swertz; and the rest of the crew step on board an alien craft, where a group of rival Globule-ites slide over, grudgingly, to make way for us interlopers.

Walking up the aisle, there's some good-natured ribbing—*Get off the bus, Gus!*—a palpable Jets-versus-Sharks tension in the air. Being one of the rare solos on the trip, I have to sit beside a stranger, and pucker my buttocks to try to take up as little seat space as possible. As soon as we get underway, my seatmate, in a voice barely loud enough for anyone but me to hear, begins whisper-singing in the dark. *"One hundred bottles of Zyklon B on the wall, one hundred bottles of Zyklon B, take one down and spray it around, ninety-nine bottles of Zyklon B"* . . . and so on.

I look around to see if anyone else has heard. But the lights are off. All I can make out in the dark is the streetlit penumbra of a large, round face. Was the tune for *my* benefit? Was the bus itself full of Weird Al Yankovic wannabe white supremacists? In my semi–dream state, I think my neighbor Round-face is singing a little louder, and imagine I hear an appreciative chuckle from the faceless riders fore and aft. I crane around, trying to spy Shlomo, my road dog, but no luck. I can't see.

What breed of Aryan race warriors have I stumbled onto? Are there, perhaps, legions of future QAnon America Firsters touring the camps the way hard-core Disney fans hit Orlando, and Anaheim, and Tokyo Disneyland? To taste all the joy the world has to offer?

Once the singing stops—or so, to my still jet-lagged, stress-bent senses, it seems—the music's replaced by loud, deliberate, accusatory sniffing. "What's that smell?" Sniff, sniff. "Can somebody open a window?"

The same not-so-subtle slur I first heard in grade school, when my PE teacher, Tank Reddin, ignited early paranoia about being Jewish by wrinkling his nose, waving a large white hanky, and muttering, "Somethin' stinks," whenever he looked my way in Hygiene. But maybe that's fake news. Feelings, as the late Hubert Selby Jr. liked to say, aren't facts. Projection, meet self-obsessed fear.

When we stop outside the fancy Kraków Sofitel hotel, and lights go on in the bus, I realize I had not been sitting beside a large-headed anti-Semite ogre at all, but a bubby from New Jersey, big round hair wrapped in a babushka held down with bobby pins. She pokes my arm, smiles benignly in my direction. "Looks like somebody had a pierogi nap. You were mumbling in your sleep." Here she pats my hand, leaving her liver-spotted paw on mine for an extra second before adding, "I hope you don't mind I opened a window." Then, with a discreet giggle, lowering her voice, "One of the fellows up front has been giving us the gas!"

So wait, nobody was saying I smelled? In my haze, I just heard it that way, because it fit the contours of that way-back, grade-school-embedded racial shame. (There, I said it.) Are you a self-hating Jew if the self you're hating was shaped by the way strangers reacted to you? From my earliest awareness, being a Jew made me nervous. I was in awe of Jews who'd grown up among Jews and never suffered for it. When I was shipped to Hebrew school, with actual fellow Jews in Jewish communities, I felt just as self-conscious among them. Worried they were going to demand my Jew card.

Even with the Bluesmart bleeping, I know I'm going to sleep tonight!

# CHAPTER 6
## *REVENGE OF THE KRAKÓW SOUP-COUGHER*

🚐 🚐 🚐

NEXT ON THE PROGRAM—breakfast at 0700!—is the Schindler museum, located in what was formerly Oskar Schindler's Enamel Factory at 4 Lipowa Street in Kraków.

On the way, our guide waxes ecstatic on the merits of Spielberg's movie on the subject, which inspired more than one of my Holocaust compadres to come along on this journey, to get to know the Jews. Here, not for the last time, I'm faced with the dilemma of knowing a tad more than the guide, giving rise to the perpetual conundrum: pipe up and risk sounding like a know-it-all dick, or hold my mud, maybe bend the ear of whatever unlucky Globuloid is nearest, and limit the know-it-all dickishness to an audience of one.

My own secret knowledge is not, strictly speaking, about the heroic Liam Neeson–portayed Oskar Schindler. It was absolutely and admirably true that Schindler, the Kraków businessman, really did persuade SS bigwigs to let him employ a thousand or so Jews in his enamel factory, let said employees live in a camp within a camp in a place called Płaszów, and single-handedly save their lives. No, what got me was sitting there having to listen to Steven Spielberg being talked about like the messiah (or at least a mensch-iah). When I knew, from the words of a dead Czechoslovakian director and Holocaust survivor, Juraj Herz, that he was a thief.

I understand, of course, that neither Suzannah nor the Spielberg-inspired bus-people have heard of Juraj Herz. But according to Herz, Spielberg had seen his work, even if he didn't know it. In fact, from the day *Schindler's List* dropped till the day he died, Herz protested Spielberg's artistic lifting. One of his film's most memorable scenes, in which a group of female prisoners mistake an actual shower for a gas chamber, was copied frame by frame from Herz's own 1986 movie, *Zastihla mě noc*. Think about how that feels. Herz said he wanted to sue, but was unable to come up with the money to fund the effort.

Here is Herz (tip of the hat to director Stephen Sayadian) discussing it all in the Czech film magazine *Kinoeye*. (Forgive me for obsessing, but somehow I relate to the late director, though I never met him.) Anyway, listen: "[This] scene in Spielberg's film doesn't make any sense. I had two main characters in the showers, but in *Schindler's List* this is just an unrelated episode. I read the novel *Schindler's List*, and there is no such scene. I asked for the script and there is also no scene like that there. I met an American lawyer and I sent him my scene and Spielberg's scene on videotape. He responded to me with a question: Why did I send him one scene from *Schindler's List* twice? When I explained to him the situation, he told me that I will win the lawsuit for sure, but I would have to put into it a hundred or two hundred thousand dollars. I would get the money back, but I would have to have it in the beginning. So I had to leave it. Spielberg is well-known for this kind of stealing. He had lawsuits with almost every film."

To quote Grandma Essie again, who knew?

(Author's note: Philip Gourevitch wrote that "*Schindler's List* depicts the Nazis' slaughter of Polish Jewry almost entirely though German eyes." Art Spiegeleman hated it. And my fave critic, Liel Leibovitz, who has *S.L.* last on his ranking of Jewish films for *Tablet*, put it this way: "The movie, really, is about a Christlike gentile who saves a horde of hapless Jews who have no agency or resolve of their own." Making it, if I may continue to lift, not just one of the most ham-handed Holocaust films ever made but also, peculiarly, one of the least Jewish in sensibility. It's not the writing, for the record, it's the premise you have to buy into. The writer involved has done spectacular scripts for everything from *Searching for Bobby Fischer* to *The Falcon and the Snowman* to *The Irishman*. He also offered to give me a car about thirty years ago, when I barely knew him. Great guy!)

All movies are of their time (the cowriter of *Bad Boys 2* says portentously). Let's not even get into the Schindler Effect, wherein tourists visit the movie's locations, or ride a bus past the hotel Spielberg stayed in. As opposed to, well, you know . . . actually visiting the actual camp.

None of which, needless to say, is Oskar Schindler's fault. Happily—if happily is the word—the museum bearing his name is designed as such a brilliant and disturbingly immersive experience that by the time my fellow bus-folk and I make it out the other side, we feel like we've survived something ourselves. If that was the goal of the exercise, the creators have succeeded beyond measure.

A minute after entering, the visitor is plunged into

sinister gloom, then forced to trudge over cobblestones—
like the very ghetto streets into which the Nazis crammed
and starved local Jews—before the terrifying sound of
barking German shepherds is blasted in, all designed to
generate a sense of the real, unbearable oppression those
souls alive and trapped in the ghetto had to endure. Before
the Nazis de-gentiled and walled the place, the ghetto was
home to three thousand. Somehow, Schindler's museum
manages to evoke the sensation of hideously cramped and
savage life when the Nazis blew that number up to seventeen thousand.

As we absorb these sensory horrors, the particulars
of oppression—how, say, Jewish professors were banned
from universities, and Jewish children banned from
schools—are projected on screens and fleshed out in displays with a beautifully claustrophobic immediacy.

Extra credit to the Schindler design team who made
the decision to portray citizens of the ghetto, living in
their tiny spaces, as spooky white mannequin figures. It's
hard to overstate the impact of these ghostly statues, the
sense of faceless, constricted menace.

A handsome café awaits the Schindler visitors who
make it to the end of the display and find themselves feeling peckish. Here I learn, not for the last time, that the
Polish are unapologetic food-coughers. The woman behind the counter makes a point of hacking point-blank
into my tomato soup. (And why not a bowl of blood after
working up an appetite sauntering through yet another
display of the Third Reich's love affair with Jew murder?)
A group of high school guys are hanging out, three of
them taking up two tables, man-spreading, just like young

Americans do. After the first cough, I don't react; anybody can get a tickle in their throat and spaz-hack. It happens. The second time, the kohl-eyed young Schindler server hocks again. Then she lets out her third and last cough, eyes locked on mine as she spits.

On the wall behind us is a reproduction of a poster for Nazi Youth. Featured are strapping pale-haired lads in short pants, who might be the ancestors of the Aryan homeboys chilling in the café beside me. Done coughing, the young lady shares a smirk—or so I imagine—with her audience of high schoolers, the fellas not that much younger than her. It isn't exactly like she spat in my bowl; it isn't that different either. But it could have been worse. She might have spit in my face.

What to do? There are times in life when you need to make a choice. And I make the choice now to take my nakedly coughed-on tray, carry it to the table of smirky high schoolers, set it down, and walk out. I'm not sure exactly what message I'm sending. But it is done quietly. With dignity. And none of the drama of, say, throwing the bowl to the floor and screaming, *Jews are people too!* You can't make people like you.

The next morning, for no apparent reason, my fellow riders appear to me in that same affectless white as the ciphers in the Schindler museum. Signifying what, I can't tell. It's still early days. But I feel, how to put this, not just disturbed—I am not just having bad weird dreams at what we've been seeing (as who wouldn't)—but somehow ashamed for seeing it. A phrase from Jewish American novelist Stanley Elkin comes to mind. Somewhere in his masterpiece *The Dick Gibson Show*, a beleaguered charac-ter cries, "Go ahead, make carnival with my pain!"

It might be argued there was something private about the suffering of the non–master races, and rolling in by bus to gawk at the scenes of the crime does not seem en-tirely, I don't know, kosher. Do the dead want an audi-ence? Surely, if I'm one of the Six Million, my crumbling bones are thinking, when the tourists trudge in, *Where were you when I needed you?*

In the actual Kraków Ghetto, we're handed off to a lo-cal guide, Tessa, a worldly older lady (and by older, I mean we could have been in tenth grade at the same time) with the classy seen-it-all panache of a Polish Bea Arthur. She shepherds us into the Remuh Synagogue. To get in, you pay fifty zlotys to a grumpy middle-aged shlub with a two-day growth eating his lunch—crustless tuna on white and a canned Coke—who takes the coins without looking up and slides over a cardboard box full of baby-blue yarmulkes.

My first thought is *head lice*, and my hand freezes half-way up to my head. (This was, of course, pre-COVID; be-fore head lice seemed like a happy distraction.) "Ve clean 'em," Cousin Grumpy says, reading my mind without looking up, and I go ahead and slap on the Yahweh doily. (Two hours ago, here in Los Angeles, a stranger deliver-ing groceries burst into tears on my front porch. Eight in the morning. "I got lost," he sputtered, a skinny man of forty, between sobs, "I can't focus anymore." "It's okay," I tell him—from a safe distance, with a mask on—"I can't either." Then I give him a glass of water. After he leaves, I throw the glass in the trash and Bactine my hands. It's nice to get the chance to be human again.)

The Kraków synagogue dates from 1553 and still has the original door, an impressive wooden slab which Tessa insists we all stop to admire.

"Sturdy," declares Don, the studly old state trooper, holding hands tightly with his partner Mariko, the elegant judicial office manager. I can't look at either without succumbing to blurt-shame, recalling our first meeting over Polish vittles. *My dad committed suicide, what's your name?* (Do you ever just wonder what is wrong with you? Anybody?) Officer Don looks my way as he speaks, and I nod back.

"Definitely sturdy," I agree, and give the wood a solid knock.

Just a couple of guys talking door sturdiness. The way guys do.

I wish I'd prepped more, perhaps on the fine points of fifteenth-century synagogue design. Next time.

# CHAPTER 7
## *GET CARTER*

🚌 🚌 🚌

THERE IS SOME DRAMA TODAY when a certain older Jewish fellow, my pal Shlomo, asks Mariko if she knows any good Chinese restaurants. Steam does not shoot out of her ears, but close. Instead she maintains an icy calm and answers simply: "First of all, I've never been to Kraków. So how would I know any restaurants? Second"—voice rising a little—"I'm Japanese, Sylvan!"

There's a tense silence. I watch the woman's slow burn. Admire her for managing a smile, doing no more than shake her head. More bemused than angry. (Or so I think.) Nothing but class.

"What did I say?" Shlomo asks, with a baffled shrug. "Did I say something?"

"What do you think?" Mariko snaps, finally showing she's human, and not saint. "Just because I have slanted eyes I can find Chinese restaurants? Like I've got some kind of built-in eggroll detector? I don't even like eggrolls."

"Sor-ry," Shlomo sulks. After this, there's free time for folks to pop out for snacks or souvenirs.

When Shlomo decides to stay in, I feel like I should keep him company. He turns to me. "How was I supposed to know?" Luckily, we're the only people on the bus.

Shlomo still cannot grok his faux pas. "I mean, she does have slanted eyes, doesn't she?"

I consider trying to explain. Is it ever too late to try to put a dent in racism? Then Shlo continues, really wrestling with himself, "I'm not a bigot, Jer. I like the yellows! And I love eggrolls. What's wrong with that?"

At which point, to my eternal shame, I punt. I could try to explain "the yellows" is not the term you want to go with. Maybe talk about judging each person by who they are, not whether or not they have an epicanthic fold. Instead, amoral coward that I am, I find myself reassuring the sweet old racist: "It's okay, buddy. But if I were you, I'd just drop it. Maybe remember we're all Americans."

"What?" Shlo makes a face at me. The man may be eightysomething, but he can still tell I'm full of shit. "That doesn't even sound like something you'd say."

"You're right, I'm a hypocrite. You're an ignorant old fart."

"That's why we're pals" he says, and gives me a belchy kiss on the forehead just as Mariko steps back on the bus. For a second our eyes meet, then she looks away. Apparently Shlomo has the same thought I do. "That's not a gay kiss, honey. It's just friendly."

Honey.

Mariko doesn't respond. Just moves up the aisle and sets her large paper bag down on the seat beside her. I can only hope it is full of wooden Jews.

There are no African Americans on the tour. And, in those pre-BLM days, I am not sure anyone (any Caucasian, that is) was enlightened enough to even notice the nonstop whiteness. My own sense is that everyone would be welcome. The demarcation here is class—specifically the middle—not race. More or less. And then Shlomo, God bless him, raises his shoulders in a textbook Michael Lerner in *Barton Fink* meshuggener shrug, toddles up to Mariko's row, and taps her on the shoulder. "Listen, hon, no hard feelings, okay? My wife and I go to PF Changs every Sunday."

After we have a peek around the inside of the synagogue, admiring the five-hundred-year-old bimah and pews, we follow Tessa back outside. She leads us up a short well-trod path to a leafy, adjoining graveyard.

"Now then," our Kraków expert begins, "let me tell you about this marvelous cemetery. The ground you're standing on is full of famous rabbis going back to the sixteenth century."

As she talks, I wonder idly what the dead rabbi in the grave to my right would make of Marvin, a porky bald insurance man from our group, now tying his orange Nike on the late holy man's tombstone.

"The Germans blew up every synagogue in Kraków. So why didn't they blow up this one?" Tessa lowers her voice, as if Gestapo were crouched on the other side of the wall. "Because the rabbi told them the earth beneath it was cursed. So instead of exploding it, the Nazis stole everything and stored equipment in the temple. Old wagons. Ammunition. Even hay. But they didn't completely spare the graveyard. In fact, they paved the road out of Kraków with broken tombstones. After the war, remaining Jews found as many gravestones as they could and put them back in the cemetery. And they're still finding them."

(On the subject of graves, we learn, in a visual signifier typical of the Nazi's subtle messaging, the actual walls
of the ghetto were constructed to resemble lines of tombstones, side to side.)

Worshippers—maybe the better word is mourners—
leave messages on scraps of paper for legendary rebbes
like Moses Israelus, a beloved sixteenth-century rabbi
whom some believe can solve their problems.

"Does he take e-mail?" cracks Tad, ever the in-bus
joker, who today favors a yarmulke over a Marlins cap.
"And take your fat foot off the tombstone, Marv. It's
dis-goddamn-respectful. How'd you like some dirty dog
feet all up on your hell-stone after you go?"

Marvin, for his part, seems genuinely contrite. "My
shoe was untied," he says weakly. And then, "Hell-stone?"
I wondered about that one myself.

Their fun little exchange over, Tessa continues: "Now,
you'll notice that scattered atop the graves are pebbles and
rocks. Christians put flowers on graves, Jews put rocks.
Why? Because when Moses led his people out of Egypt,
people died. They would bury them in the desert and put
stones on them. There's a saying in Hebrew, 'Putting down
stones, we always remember.'"

A beautiful story. And as she finishes, I'm impressed
all over again at the particular humane genius of the way
this tour is set up. The arc of it. Memorials and ghettos are
like painful-but-sadly-beautiful urban hors d'oeuvres. A
civilized way to ease into uglier, more hellish destinations
to come. I resolve, if things keep going south in the States,
to return to Kraków and see about making a humble living yanking weeds and arranging stones on the graves in

this tiny cemetery. It feels, for the moment, like the most deeply satisfying avocation on the planet. There's an aura of heavy peace about the place I can't put my finger on, but that persists throughout the journey. Something like: The worst that can happen here has already happened. Or maybe just: Relax, death is only the beginning, if you die in the right place.

I'm not sure why, but I would love to have people slip me questions after I'm dead and buried. But I suppose, like Moses Israelus, you've got to earn the honor. And put up with rando Nikes.

(Interesting side note, on the subject of Kraków, there seem to be a fair amount of full-on punks, or punk manqués, roaming the city stenciling the iconic image of a shotgun-wielding Michael Caine, from the original *Get Carter*, on any available alley wall. One mohawked fellow, seeing me watching, turns to give me the Polish finger. It's almost like home! I have yet to discern the meaning of Caine's cool-ass image to disaffected Kraków youth, or if they are even disaffected. For all I know, they're just fans of seventies British noir. In which case, hats off to you, young Poland, for excellent taste in cinematic graffiti.)

# CHAPTER 8
## A BRIEF DIGRESSION
### ("MEET THE JEWGINA!")

🚌 🚌 🚌

FOR A COUPLE OF MINUTES, EARLY ON, I had the truly revolting idea to try and use Alt.Com, haven for so-called alternative sexual practices, to delineate the various perversions peculiar to each camp's nearby environs. Not that I'm into this kind of thing. God no! It was strictly anthropology.

Was Oświęcim, say, a haven for spank-action? It would make some kind of sense. But who knows what descendants of Auschwitz-ville were really into? Der führer, they say, was somewhat of a scathound. Allegedly (of course) he went to brown-town with Eva Braun, a generation before Danny Thomas invented the plate job. (Comedy buffs who know, know.) And all this before "insurrectionists" emptied their bowels on Nancy Pelosi's carpet.

Adolf and Eva, those crazy kids, got hitched the same day they suicided in the bunker. Whether or not Hitler's last-minute missus could actually defecate in the shape of swastikas—a Weimar party trick involving turkey baster, cake mold, and practice—has never been verified. Tough call. Where I grew up the big industries were steel and beer. Near Auschwitz, back in the day, it was death and torture. Who knows what that does to the locals—then or now. Imagine: *Honey, I'm home! Time for Bundt cake and coprophagia! And bring those pix of Great-Grandpa Helmut in his Waffen-SS gear!*)

I just signed on to the site long enough to try and pin things down. The way it works, each country is broken into regions. In each region, you can see the number of locals who describe themselves as devotees of this or that erotic predilection. Sadly—or strangely—or sadly and strangely, it turns out Poland has no branch of Alt.com. So all my speculation about Auschwitz-adjacent deviance turns out to be completely unfounded.

Boy is my face red! The Polish national slogan is *Bóg, Honor, Ojczyzna* (God, Honor, Fatherland). Though it could, just spitballing here, be *Milli Ludzie! Normalny Seks! Smaczna Kielbasa!* (Nice People! Normal Sex! Tasty Sausage!) Which, it turns out, is not the only lesson to be learned. "Coprophagia"—who knew?—was not just an erstwhile top Nazi party fetish, it is also the name of a product made by the NaturVet company, a canine-stool-eating deterrent—plus breath freshener. World of wonders.

Germany, unlike its neighbor to the east, is broken into fifteen Alt.com sections, from Bavaria to the free state of Thuringia. (Birthplace, I shudder to think, of Thuringer, the weird lunch-meat combo of beef tongue and pork blood that Mama Trish, our babysitter, made me and my sister eat on Wonder Bread, with mayo and relish. She also gave me ringworm when we "cuddled." Things were different then.)

In Bavaria, home of Dachau, in late 2016 you might have found thirty-four pony play devotees. Plus eighty-one verbal abuse fans. Go figure.

Of course, the whole exercise was pointless and stupid. But also, it might be said, informative and fraught with as much import as you want it to be. Does it mean anything that fifty-seven male Buchenwald-adjacents, down Weimar way, enjoy playing Adult Babies? Drinkers or Stinkers, depending. (It might be 5,700, but my notes are smudged, and that sounds like a lot.) Side issue: the truly avant thing about erstwhile Nazi towns is that you can be walking down any ho-hum street when, wedged among a dress shop, schnitzel stand, and auto parts outlet, you're face-to-face with a storefront marked *Sado-Maso* (which could, arguably, employ all three).

I speak from personal experience. An unnamed spouse and I once wandered into a family-run Berlin sado parlor and, Bob's your uncle, ten minutes later she was hanging upside down getting naked feather-dusted by a switch named Magda. While Mom sat in back, watching *Knight Rider* in German. (Germany still loves the Hoff!)

That Dachau locals, and this is the last I'll say about it, go in for rubberwear and humiliation makes its own weird sense. But ultimately, of course, it's bad science. Bunk sociology. And an idea I dropped. Only mentioned as evidence of your author's occasionally impaired judgment. What can happen when you don't sleep, you're sundowning, and your Internet works in Eastern Europe.

Okay, I did have one online encounter. About which all I can say is, I could not (and God knows would not) have invented it. And God knows why I'm marching it out now.

In order—did I mention?—to make myself privy to the perv stats above, I had to sign on to the site and make believe I was some kind of pervaloid myself. What a stretch! I came up with the nom de perv *Mean Daddy 50*, and listed my propensity for, I don't quite recall exactly, something bland like spanking. (After *Fifty Shades of Grey*, everything but drawing-and-quartering feels vaguely corny.)

Anyway, I'm in the Warsaw Hilton, fighting insomnia, the night before I'm supposed to go to my first death camp, when I got a notice that I had a, what's the word—suitor? cum buddy? subby pen pal?—DMing me. What the hell? My, um, let's go with supplicant, whose online handle was *Special Need*, describes herself as wanting a very particular kind of verbal abuse. When I DM, *What kind of verbal abuse?* I get back, *Tell me you'd slap and hurt my filthy Jewish vagina!* Which sounds like a Jackie Mason routine, if Jackie Mason worked blue.

In an earlier book, quick flashback, I chronicled the story of a German girlfriend who, when we went to bed, would work herself up screaming, "Nein! Nein! Nein! I'm being fucked by a Jew!" Playing her, in the movie version, Connie Nielsen simply couldn't, or wouldn't, belt it out at top volume. Compared to Hebraic vagina slaps, that was Bible college.

I felt so uncomfortable, I got whatever is the opposite of an erection. A doorbell?

*Oh! Oh!* I am suddenly reading. *Hurt my nasty Jewish Vagina! Are you going to hurt it? Are you going to slap my bad vagina!*

*Yes, yes!* I type, out of sheer boredom, and here I make my first mistake. Bad vagina just sounds so English-as-a-second-language, I thought I'd spice it up. Y'know, get creative. Like, *Okay, get ready! I'm going to smack that nasty Jew-hole!*

Which prompted, weirdly (as if anything could be *more* weird) the indignant response, *That's gross! Just hurt my dirty Jewgina!*

"Jewgina?" I hear myself say out loud. But there's no stopping now. Special Need is typing up a storm.

*Hit it! Hurt it! Spank my vagina really hard!*

And yes, I do feel ridiculous. Worse, now *I* feel dirty. Am I turned on? Jesus . . . There's no accounting for taste, so I go ahead and type: *Get ready! I'm going to spank your bad Jewish vagina! Right now, I'm smacking it. Smack smack smack! I'm really hurting it! BAD BAD BAD!*

Which, to my surprise, elicits the mini–Molly Bloom-ish stream-of-consciousness, *Yes yes YES! Bad bad bad! OHHHHHH YESSSSS! I'm cumming! YESSSSSSSSSSSSSSS!*

Over and out. The whole thing was, to say the least, surreal. And, to say even less, infinitely more disturbing than arousing. On the other hand, hey, sometimes you just want to be of service.

Reading this, I think, can you blame ridiculous and ill-considered ideas on depression? Jet lag? Early demen-tia? I'm going to say no. But only to virtue signal, *Look, I'm cutting myself no slack here!* Do you get a pass if you have to chain yourself to the bedstand to keep from diving out your hotel window?

No again. But never mind. I've got to get some sleep.

Tomorrow it's off to Auschwitz.

# CHAPTER 9
## COMFORTABLE SHOES

🚌 🚌 🚌

"I HOPE YOU ARE ALL IN COMFORTABLE SHOES for Auschwitz. We've got a lot of walking. And we're behind schedule."

Well, yes! Because when you think Auschwitz, you think comfortable shoes. Or you do if you're our tour guide, Suzannah, and you want to make sure nobody in your charge succumbs to death camp bunions.

This practical worry catches me off guard, but I shouldn't be surprised. This is the woman's job. Visit enough genocide sites and genocide sites are bound to become normal. In the end it's always a battle between personal comfort and psycho-historical horror.

Whether your feet hurt or not, as I'm soon to learn, horror wins. Just not necessarily for the reasons you think.

As it happens, on the way to Auschwitz we go through Częstochowa, home of the Black Madonna. This icon of the Virgin Mary, allegedly painted on a table used by the Holy Family, attracts throngs of faithful. The Black Madonna is said to have cured illness, granted wishes, and, most intriguing, made her own theft impossible by becoming progressively heavier. (Been there!) At this rate the shrine of the Holy Mother will have to be wheeled out in a purring Scamper, like members of the 400-Plus Club at the Decatur Mall, who meet every Friday in front of the second floor Cinnabon. (*Let's go Scamp-draggin'!*)

Of more historical significance, the icon protected Poles from marauding Swedes in 1655, and later appeared in the sky over the Vistula River and freaked out an invading Russian army so much they turned around and marched back to the steppes.

All in all, the Holy Mother is a celebrated protector of Polish souls. Unless, of course, the souls belonged to Polish Jews. According to my late grandfather Moishe—one of those guys who couldn't read but could tell you 317 x 51,564 in two seconds—the goyim liked to cap off a good Madonna pilgrimage with impromptu pogroms, your basic postsalvation anti-Semitic killing spree. Often on horseback. Moishe grew up in this city, and escaped at sixteen to avoid recruitment in the czar's army. And this, of course, was before Germans rolled in and set up camps, to take the guesswork out of Jew-death.

I wonder if it's worth sneaking off-tour to visit the Black Madonna shrine. Maybe it *can* work miracles. But what to ask for? Reprieve from the whole insanity-depression-and-suicidal-ideation package, or DACA relief? The eternal question. Side by side, I'd say the Dreamers deserve the miracle.


As I write this now—in the present—I should point out that these last few days have been, well, tricky, on the free-floating-despair front. Is quarantine pink eye a thing? Psycho-emotional pink eye?

*I can't go on, I'll quote Samuel Beckett.*

It's been a challenge, diving back into the past in these pages. I have, in fact, been FDOM for a few twenty-four hours. Facedown on the Mattress. F. Scott Fitzgerald said, famously, "In a real dark night of the soul it is always three o'clock in the morning." Maybe. But, speaking personally, three in the afternoon packs much more of a face-in-the-mirror-screaming–"What happened?" opportunity than three in the morning. But that's me.

Shut up and write, white man.

Election Day 2020 now seems like the quaint past. In the centuries since, the now ex-president continues to make "I won by a landslide" noises. Despite, of course, not winning.

"There's a lot of frustration behind closed doors in the president's orbit," CNN tells us, what with the whole insurrection and government-overthrow thing. I've got frustration of my own, as it happens. I don't have a TV. (Or a couch, for that matter. We're keeping the just-moved-in feel going as long as possible.) The good news, I've just discovered: you can stream CNN or MSNBC online. The bad news, on my little iPad it cuts out a lot, and sometimes comes back in Korean. Or what I think is Korean.

"I'm worried the situation could get dangerous," says conservative ex-senator Rick Santorum on CNN. A man, let's not forget, so opposed to abortion, he took the corpse of his stillborn baby home from the hospital to cuddle for a couple of weeks. 'Cause that's how a Christian family rolls. Or his Christian family. Who also, for all I know, brings deceased grandparents back home for a postdead spooning before going in the ground. 'Cause it's a nice way to send them off. Necro-spooning is not (yet) one of the categories on Alt.com. At least I don't think. I have not—mea culpa—put enough time studying the ins and outs.

In the end I skipped the Black Madonna experience—and her chance at healing—but on the way to Auschwitz deleted five messages from my WGA insurance doctor at the Bob Hope Medical Center without listening to them. (And yes, it is a tad hard to take seriously any life-and-death info that comes from an establishment named for the Nixon-friendly comedian and star of *"Boy, Did I Get a Wrong Number!"* Separate issue . . .) The doctor had results, answers to the mystery mass on my kidney. Which I came to think of as my own little tumor child. Perhaps, if and when it's removed, I too would take the little lump home for a cuddle, like role model and family values zealot Rick Santorum. Whose sweater vests alone could make you a Muslim. But I believe the Madonna guided my fingers. The beauty of the Divine is that it's indecipherable. Not unlike Polish itself, which is not only impossible to understand, but painful.

To my untrained ear, the Polish language sounds like the kind of noise, say, that emanates from one toilet stall over in a Port Authority men's room, where you think it's someone gagging on a penis, but turns out to be just a stranger taking a highly emotional bowel movement. (Not that English, to the Polish, must sound any better.)

The roughness of the language strikes me again as I'm being hectored outside a McDonald's rest stop in Częstochowa. I stop to take a photo—but no sooner do I aim my iPhone than a Rondo Hatton–esque (google him, it's worth it) Polish lad, and his equally imposing buddies, quickly materialize.

It's New York in the 1970s all over again, facing the fist-in-your-teeth glare of aggro urbanites, in this case holding it down at an Eastern European Mickey D's. They'd made a show of leaping up from their table to step outside and stand in front of me with matching crossed arms, like rappers in some old-school hip-hop video.

*Well hey*, I have to bite my tongue to keep from blurting, *maybe one of you has a great-great-grandfather who horsewhipped my great-great-grandfather. Or maybe he raped my great-great-grandmother! We could be related!*

Just something to chill things out.

The whole posse wears the green and white of what I guess is a football club: the White Eagles. (Later I learn, because I'm a fucking idiot, that White Eagles are not a football club. White Eagles is the name of what they call the Fascist Party over there, like the Boogaloos or Q in the good old US of A.)

The Rondo doppelgänger steps to me, three inches from my face, before barking, "Yo, Jew-tard? Why are you taking our picture?"

(Full disclosure: Long before being set upon by Polish burger thugs, I had McDonald's issues. I'd worked there, not to brag, at the ripe age of thirty-eight, and had to endure the whispered comments of my co-employees—most of whom were seventeen—all boiling down to a single, incredulous observation as they gazed surreptitiously my way: "I think he's retarded." With the Black Madonna McDonald's torment, I feel I've come full circle.)

A few lads pick up the chant and *Jew-tard* me. For one bad moment I think, insanely, maybe they're not heckling me, maybe I'm being jumped in. (Okay, I'm lying, the second big Pole may not have said *Jew-tard*. It was, if you want to parse, maybe closer to *Juden*. But I could have been overthinking. Before I could figure it out, the fellas switched it up to Żydowskie szumowiny. Which, Shlomo explained later, means *Jewish toilet scum*. More or less. Harsh as it is, you have to admit it's damply expressive.)

The Rondo Hattan leader barks in what I guess is Kraków gangster argot, "Turn your dimple ass around." (How does he know?) As he shouts, I take the only defense that ever worked for me. Looking hard. Fronting. I can look reasonably tough, with absolutely nothing to back it up. (The problem, and it's a genetic thing, is that I can also, without meaning to, creep people out by wearing this same face in situations of friendly banter, or the awkward silent parts of business meetings. It's what my older daughter used to call my "hate face." The one I was born with. A great mug for staving off wolf pack attacks on the three a.m. IRT uptown in 1974 Manhattan. But a burden in situations of normal socializing, when the last vibe you want to convey is offended and mean. Or worse, inappropriately hostile.)

"Turn around and go. Vamoot!" the young wanna-thug repeats.

It's here that I catch myself saying, in defusal mode, "Bro, I'm not taking a picture of you, just the McDonald's. That's what I do." For a second my apex predator opponent's eyes shrink to slits, in what I take is angry uncertainty. I press the advantage and repeat, "I'm just a McDonald's photographer. That's what I do. That's my job! I travel the world snapping the Golden Arches."

I shrug, give the universal *Hey, it's a gig* gesture. Just a couple of dudes shooting the Eastern European breeze. "You know, for the zlotys," I continue, employing the same Dale Carnegie principle that inspired Charlie Manson: always talk about something the other guy can relate to.

What am I, a collaborator? An appeaser?

I get (not surprisingly) nothing from David Dukeowsky over here. I want to punch myself in the face.

Giant trans-Poland semis slam by on the motorway. The leader just looks at me through his reflector shades and spits.

Not at me. But close enough that when I smile, it's creepy. Again, Screaming Eagle grins for a second. His teeth are better than mine. Then he steps forward and launches a sudden left-pec chest-bump that comes up from his toes and knocks me back. At which point, two thoughts hit me at once. One, it looks like things are about to go Full Pogrom. Two, being the victim of a hate crime in Poland is a pretty good story. Think Hunter Thompson getting his ass kicked by Hells Angels. (Which this situation in no way resembles. But, sort of?)

So maybe I should lean into it. In the movie version I would say something like, *You want a piece of this Jew ass, you're gonna have to take it, pardner*. In actual life, I just hold that creepy smile. Don't say a word. And before either Rondo the Fascist Eagle or I can do anything further, who strolls into frame but Shlomo, Big Mac in one hand and a Coke in the other. He gestures with his burger hand. "What are you doing? We're late!" Then, in a lower voice, he turns to the Screaming Eagles and adds, "Obszcymurek." Which backs them up fast.

I follow without looking back, not even when Shlomo stops slurping from his straw long enough to spit over his shoulder and keep walking.

"What did you call him?" I ask.

"Obszcymurek. It means, in English, sort of 'punk' or 'piece of shit.' It's very Polish. Anyway, you can't reason with a Cossack," he says matter-of-factly.

"Neo-Nazis . . . You forget they're not all in MAGA hats."

"Neo-shmeeo. They're Nazis, like their fathers before them."

"Jesus, Shlomo."

I regard the man with new respect. Behind that facade of clueless old-guyishness is a total badass. I guess you don't survive being orphaned, tossed in a DP camp, and shipped to a country on your own at nine without picking up some survival skills.

We walk a little bit up the highway to a gas station. Inside, after we both use the men's room—one zloty!—I go out front and spot Shlomo eyeballing a Polish *Playboy* in the magazine rack. I put a hand on his sloping shoulder and thank him. "You saved my bacon."

Shlomo snorts. "Kosher bacon, boychick. In case you haven't walked by a mirror lately, you can't pass."

"Well, thank you anyway. Who knows what could have happened?"

"Accch. It's nothing. Forget it."

But back on the bus, the incident seems to have revived him. "Couple of New York Yids," he crows, sounding a little giddy. "They're gonna mess with a couple of

New York Yids? I don't think so. We ain't all little sisi pu-tzes." Then he gets serious again, reaching up to huddle and place his hands on my shoulder, his voice low. "You do know you look Jewish, right? We're in Poland."

Soon enough, the ribbing begins.

"Well, well," Tad pipes up as we step by him, down the aisle. "I heard somebody had to save Gerald from some real tough customers. Local muscle!" To punctuate the point, Tad leans out and gives Shlo a squeeze on the back of his knee. "Pretty slick, Sylvan."

At first Shlomo doesn't reply. He's too dignified. But when he gives his mom jeans an extra tug, up over the gentle slope of his tummy—he wears them high, closer to nips than navel—I know he's feeling it. The up-tug, I've come to learn, is his tell. When tickled, or excited, Shlo grabs his belt and yanks his old-guy mommers north. I can't help but smile at the inches of shiny ankle now visible over my old new friend's tennis shoes. (Keds!)

"Back in Texas," Madge claps, "you're what we'd call one tough hombre."

Another tug of those mom jeans, and I can tell Shlo-mo's loving it. I chime in: "The man's being modest. He would have wiped the sidewalk with those delinquents. Busted some kind of Hebrew fighting moves. I've never seen anything like it."

"*Jew*-jitsu!" Shlomo clucks. "Get it?" I love hearing him giggle at his own joke. "Gerald's plenty tough on his own, let me tell you."

"Not what I heard," Madge kids, reaching past Tad to give the alta kocker's butt a squeeze. I can tell he's proud. It's a beautiful thing.

This is, for about twenty seconds, so much more fun than riding the bus in high school!

I'm still thinking about this as we pass the gingerbread houses in the quaint town of Oświęcim, along the lane to the camp. Such adorable homes. You can almost smell the scent of fresh baked cookies. During the war, apparently, the townsfolk had no idea what was going on just up the road. Except, you know, when the chimneys were going full tilt, and the hausfraus were not happy with all that foul ash. Not to mention the stench. (Tough to cover the stink of burning humans with strudel waft.)

And yes. There are so many deep, meaningful things to say about Auschwitz. About any camp. And I'd planned on stopping to contemplate them. But I'm not going to be contemplating anything right now. I need to postpone my long-imagined Auschwitz moment. Because, being a man of a certain age, the second the bus squeals to a halt, I fly out of it, gripped by such an urgent need to urinate that it is hard to be profound about anything. Except, perhaps, my vengeful prostate. (Speaking of, I should mention, due to botched back surgery while writing this book, I ended up on the table an extra three hours, as the result of which my bladder failed; I had to piss through a tube for four weeks and, until I had emergency plumbing surgery, was told I would, pardon the expression, be "wearing a bag" the rest of my life. And trust me, you haven't lived until a male nurse, formerly employed at Leavenworth, shoves a hose up your urethra, sans lube, while telling you to *Be a man!* But that's a different story for a different time. Suffice it to say, after a bad patch, I can now piss standing up, like an American.)

Perhaps it's unavoidable that, in the moment, the condition of being human, with all its attendant visceral and undignified business, does battle with the dignity of the travesty at hand. Far deeper thinkers than me have wrestled with this moral quandary. For now, I will quote just one, Mel Brooks: "Tragedy is when I cut my finger. Comedy is when you fall into an open sewer and die."

As I crane my neck for restrooms, I see a batch of other old bus bladders, sprung-shot from their motor coaches. Faces locked in that same grim, single-minded focus that makes the fact that you're about to enter the site of one of the worst crimes against humanity secondary to hoping you don't wet yourself before you get there.

I cannot even say that I feel guilty. I'm working my way up to guilt. What I feel, gripped by naked, clammy bodily need, is something else. How to put this? I've never felt more Jewish.

# CHAPTER 10

## THE MAW OF THE OVEN

🚌 🚌 🚌

FOR A FEW BAD BEATS, before we can even enter the facility, my fellow sweating seniors and I are stuck in that crowded line. Hopping from leg to leg. Around me are mooks in shorts, swells in heavy metal T-shirts. (Is the choice of Megadeth random, or unashamedly specific?) People laughing, texting, talking, staring off, doing what people do. All of it seems wrong. Where is the impact of the moment? This must be some mutant spinoff of Heisenberg's principle: Does the act of visiting a genocide site in a horde of crowded, braying tourists impact the gravitas of genocide? Is any venue even partially packed with large Americans sucking the nipples on their water bottles inherently de-gravitased? Perhaps the fallout from packaging horror for tourists—turning it to Auschwitz-land—makes a certain indignity unavoidable. The dead have no say in the matter. And I am not here to judge.

The line moves slowly and Suzannah is not happy. Due to road work, traffic had crawled, and now we are running behind. "I'm sorry," she announces as we get off the bus, "we only have an hour and fifteen minutes." I'd normally get mad, but all I can do at the news is shake my head, doubtless spewing beads of need-to-pee sweat on the people around me.

Finally, I'm through the iconic gates—*ARBEIT MACH FREI*—but need relief before I can surrender to emotion. As I fly by I remember that in 2014 the sign was stolen, but not by Nazis, and not by Jews. It was local goons. Who, for no apparent reason, cut the sign into three pieces. Possibly to sell as scrap. Possibly as a means of vile defacement. No motive was ever fully ascertained. Perhaps, who knows, a Polish fraternity prank. Like Skull & Bones initiates forced to lie naked in a coffin and spill their adolescent sex secrets to fellow Bonesmen. But with genocidal Nazi artifacts (instead of Geronimo's skull).

The vista grips you: barracks, chimney, the ground where prisoners stood for morning count each day, sometimes for hours, in the freezing cold, until they began to drop. Now weeds and grass and gravel, the ground was described by Holocaust-surviving Polish short story writer Tadeusz Borowski in *This Way for the Gas, Ladies and Gentlemen* as "nothing but leaden, shoe-swallowing mud and shit." (And anyone who has not read Borowski, please put down this book, run or scroll to your fave local bookstore or library, and treat yourself. If treat is the word for Borowski's scorching, heartbreaking, darkly hilarious prose.)

Shouldn't I be dropping to my knees? Or keening? Probably. Instead, spotting the men's room off to the right in a long low building, I bolt in—and nearly kneecap myself on the edge of a wooden card table, behind which slouches the hard-eyed bathroom attendant in a ratty blue sweater, reading a newspaper. He stares up at me like I've interrupted a state dinner.

As far I can tell, the bathroom sector is the one booming industry in Poland. From my informal research, there isn't a single unmanned toilet in the country. But it takes a minute to suss out the protocol. Am I paying admission? Or is peeing free, and the idea is you tip on the way out? Either way, from what I can tell, it's the same business model as a bridge troll's. What you are paying for is the right to pass.

After a moment, I realize I'm staring at the young toilet kommandant. And he's staring back. Glaring. Like, *Just fucking ask me, asshole. How did I end up working at a death camp crapper?* What's it like to sell piss tickets to Holocaust tourists all day? What happens to people who don't pay? Is there, perhaps, a mini-camp out back for men's room scofflaws?

Only sixty thousand out of 1.5 million survived this place. What goes through the toilet-master's mind, staring from his station at the biggest crime scene in history? Just another day in the office, except the office is in Auschwitz?

So many questions! Is he, I wonder, a fourth-generation death camp crapper hand? Had his great-great-grandfather sat where he's sitting, helping Reichsführer-SS Himmler piss when he came to visit Kommandant Höss, whose wife and children kept a lovely garden on the other side of the wall?

I start to ask, but just then a guy comes in behind me, tosses a coin in the glass bowl—not unlike the one that held yarmulkes in Kraków—and edges by me without a backward glance. Finally I go in too, and find myself fatally pee-shy. Of course! Alpha-candyass that I am, I so want to interview the attendant that I pay him again on the way out, and try to strike up a conversation.

"So . . . how'd you get into the business?"

He doesn't answer. Just scowls. Then a large man in a suede jacket strides in, sizes up the situation, and says something that sounds like "dupek" as he squeezes by me. The two men snicker like I'm not there. Thus defeated, and utterly shunned, I leave. Still needing to pee. Does it mean anything to suffer, if your suffering's voluntary? Is it helping any cause beyond bladder guilt, and my own sweaty discomfort? ("Dupek," thank you Google Translate, means "a-hole.")

This is not the experience I thought I would be having. I'm just going to say, I think Tripadvisor achieves a remarkably neutral tone here: "The toilets outside Auschwitz museum charge one zloty, inside the museum (Block 18 and behind gas chamber) are free."

Just typing the phrase—"behind gas chamber"—I wonder if the bard of Tripadvisor considered the import of his contribution. Thousands died screaming on this very ground. But hey, here's where you pee for free! I suppose, if you're going to license the nightmare, you need to factor in some relief too. Though it seems, in a way, a righteous thing that visitors should squirm in some kind of discomfort. (I think, out of nowhere, of the bit of barbed wire—the cilice—that Opus Dei members wear around their thighs to remember the Lord's suffering and atone for their own sins. And stop thinking about it when I picture William Barr's thigh. Which I don't want in my brain. How much wire is required to compensate for, say, having the DOJ represent the president in a rape case, or tear-gas BLM protesters to clear Lafayette Park for a photo op? I bet Barr's thighs are really plump. But there's horror and there's horror. As described in a *Guardian* article, the cilice "has sharp prongs that dig into the skin and flesh, though generally it does not draw blood." Nothing unreasonable.)

Still, it feels vaguely wrong that the concentration camp experience doesn't hurt. Then again, nobody's marketing actual terror and atrocity, just the experience of strolling around where terrifying atrocities were committed. The whole question exists as a sort of moral Möbius strip, with no sure footing, and every thought generating the opposite of itself. I can feel my inner Jews wrestling each other to the ground, trying to decide if we even deserve to urinate—the relief! the agony! the symbolic defilement!—if it's right or wrong to be here.

Either way, back outside something in my consciousness shifts. Until you feel your feet on the ground, and consider the dead beneath them, until you inhale, and a voice in your head asks the question only visitors to death camps ask, *Am I breathing air in which the ghost of human ush still lingers?* only then will you realize there exists but one certainty: that there is no way to comprehend the horror. And to assume you can actually dishonors those who endured it . . .

I'd lost my tour group, and decide to head for the crematorium. The only one left intact out of the five originals. It's a little crowded. In the dressing rooms outside the gas chamber, the architects, diabolically, provided hooks for inmates' clothes; each hook with a number, so inmates could find them after their shower. As if the whole operation were some sort of glorified YMCA locker room. (Which, I'm sorry, triggers memories of our recent, reluctant ex-president's farewell, get-on-the-plane-to-Mar-a-

Lago walk-off song. Long after the psycho-political fallout of the man's steroid-and-Adderall-fueled reign dissipates, the images of him rally-dancing, busting those boomer freak moves to "YMCA," may finally begin to fade. Say what you will about Hitler, the führer never got down and got funky to catchy, gay-centric Teutonic Golden Oldies.)

The SS, as the world knows, would subject new arrivals to an assignment: the able-bodied were chosen for slave labor in the camp, and the slow death of starvation, disease, overwork, and violence. The rest—the sick, the old, the feeble—were directed to the showers. Where, of course, showerheads were fake and pipes sprayed Zyklon B and doors locked behind the inmates as the death gas was released.

It is one thing to know, abstractly, how victims were told to leave their clothes and belongings before marching naked to their own death. But to see the actual changing room—to see those numbers, their plain ordinariness—is to confront the perverse theater on display on a whole new level. Those numbers, to me, were more chilling than the guard towers.

Inside, the gas chamber is as horrific (overused word) as you'd think. The stains, the airlessness, the scratch marks on the wall. Where, you imagine, people scraped with their last dying breath, trying to claw their way out . . . I obsess on those scratches. They give a hideous specificity to the unknowable.

Suddenly I hear a nasal voice: "They're not real."

"What are you talking about?" a woman replies.

I turn around, and behind me a very young, very American hipster couple is bickering.

"They rebuilt the room in 1947," the kid says, quickly setting off his partner. In a second their sniping gets louder. "The chimney's a replica too," he sniggers, like he's got one over on the Six Million. The whole time the know-it-all's lecturing, he doesn't look up from his phone. For one staggered minute I wonder if he's one of those Pokémon fanatics. Recently, the Auschwitz-Birkenau State Museum was forced to issue a statement forbidding visitors from playing Pokémon Go on their phones during visits to the former Nazi death camp. Because—they have to explain?—it is "disrespectful." Pokémon Goers are asked to abstain, but the way Hipster Boy hovers, eye-fucking his smartphone and moving in tight circles, I can't help wondering if he's not trying to capture Rattata even as we speak.

It's too much. While not usually one to meddle, I can't help myself and chime in, "Are you fucking kidding me? You're having a gas chamber fight? What is wrong with you?"

"Fuck you."

"I *am* fucked!" I hear myself snap. Well, I guess I showed him! Is that what I wanted to say?

I have to flee. That or risk being the first man to commit (or suffer) homicide at a death camp. I mean, since they closed. That I know of. Would it be all that surprising if Toilet Man doubled as cleanup killer, taking out the odd Juden or Romani tightwad who stiffs him in the can, or—forget the pee-theft—commits the ever-more-dangerous crime of NBA, Not Being Aryan? This guy would not have a job without his ancestors' genociding . . . But outside, it's worse. A combo platter of petty torment: heat, crowds, and—the memory still cringe-burns—the confused Filipina teens who mistake me for Kramer and want that selfie.

There are, in life, situations in which the opportunity for total, unhinged dickishness is so *there*, so once-in-a-lifetime, walk-through-the-door-and-be-a-shame-based-skeek-until-they-fit-your-ass-for-the-coffin irresistible, you just can't stop. Can't *not* be a dick. From then on, think regret. Think scalding, core-of-your-humanity shame, the cosmic Al Green special: a boiling pot of grits thrown on your soul—in the bathtub!—every time you ponder it. Because (it might help if you stop repeating yourself) you can't stop repeating yourself. Perseverating.

So it is, I flew nearly halfway around the world and signed on with a bus tour because I craved the up-close experience of the darkest of dark stains on humanity, and instead I'm experiencing . . . humanity. Being human. At Auschwitz. Feeling like a human stain myself. Why isn't everybody ripping the skin off their faces and biting the dirt? It occurs to me, the memorial's brass should just fence the place off and make people stare from a distance. Declare the space too toxic, like Chernobyl. Give the ghosts some fucking peace.

For a few minutes I have the crematorium to myself. The ovens are kept open, gaping, so you can see inside. The doors, built into an orange brick wall, are framed by a rectangle of brown metal. The top of the oven is round, like the tops of arches—don't even think it—framed in the shape of a giant horseshoe. The matching doors open out, in the manner of suicide doors on a '61 Lincoln. Since Ford makes Lincolns, you have to wonder if the ovens are an homage to big-time Hitler fan Henry himself.

How could they not be? It's not like any other car maker stashed anti-Semitic tracts in the glove box with the new car manual. And Hitler did not lay the Grand Cross of the German Eagle on any other CEO. Heil Henry!

The maw of each oven slopes upward at forty-five degrees. So the bodies, when fed in, were literally swallowed up. The bricks closest to the opening are coated white with what seems to be ash—though how could that be, it's been seventy years? Just under the oven, a light dusting of what at least looks like human cremains covers a battered metal table, on top of which sits a kind of squat semi-gurney, a wood plank, extending like a tongue depressor from the burned-white, giant mouth.

"You know what this looks like? It looks like a pizza oven."

No!

That smug bray. It's Fake Scratches guy, who I'd just had words with.

I stay back against the wall, facing one of the ovens, peering forward intently. I want to see nothing else, and suddenly I can't see anything at all. That passes, like a white-out, and I come to focus on the lock mechanism: a long bar running lengthwise at the front edge of the right-hand door, so it clicks home on the left. Begging the question, why was a lock necessary on an oven? Even if the bodies were already dead, apparently, they didn't want to give them the chance to escape. Third Reich Thorough. The whole mechanism—from four-inch-thick doors to horseshoe frame to metal table—owns a quality I can only describe as "hard-used." Industrial. Was it, I wonder suddenly, a two-man job? If so, what did they talk about?

Did they gossip? Did they bitch? Or did everybody just scream? Probably not. They were probably too exhausted to do anything more than the job. Not to mention, their overlords could kill them at will. Who knows? Call it empathy without insight. Because, really, who can imagine actually being there? But still . . .

For an instant, I feel a no-doubt delusional, almost out-of-body comprehension of the dead; their bodies; and those not-yet-dead who had to drag the newly dead out of the gas chambers, to see them burned. The Sonderkommandos. Prisoners who wheeled the corpses here, in return for staying out of the oven themselves a little longer.

Just staring at the furnace, thinking about that, I am consumed with the unoriginal, can-opener-in-the-heart realization that men worked and sweat in here all day, five feet from where I'm standing. Deniers have long asserted that since it takes an hour to cremate a body, the camp could never have even gotten close to the 900,000 victims historians claim. But the site hdot.org (Holocaust Denial on Trial) quotes one Henryk Tauber, a member of the Sonderkommandos: "We worked in two shifts, a day shift and a night shift. On average we incinerated 2,500 bodies a day."

That's how you do it.

In their wholly undramatic, just-the-facts-ma'am prose (which somehow make the words more powerful), hdot.org continues: "In Auschwitz-Birkenau, Nazi camp authorities were not burdened by respect for the dead or any need to consider civilian rules regarding cremation. The ovens were filled with as many bodies as could be fit into them. For instance, the men in the Sonderkommandos were instructed to combine the bodies of fat people, skeletal 'Muselmänner,' and children." Muselmänners, for non–Holocaust obsessos, were inmates in the last stages of starvation and exhaustion—inmates resigned to their own death. (Essentially, the living dead.) This method— and these victims—brought the grand total of bodies in the flames close to 1.1 million. Or 900,000. (Estimates vary.)

I am visiting this place because I want to feel the dead. But when I try to, here, I find myself thinking about the living; specifically, in this instant, the living victims enlisted to burn the dead ones.

I cannot stop imagining, on the table in front of me, a foot or two from the corpse pile on the half gurney, a swastikaed thermos of coffee, a battered canteen of schnapps, a wrapped-up bratwurst. All the extras bestowed on the future dead for doing the worst job on earth. And, as if on cue, my self-induced hallucination is ripped away and I'm plunged back into the seamy present, by actual humans. From delusions of Primo Levi to *Hogan's Heroes* in the space of a bleat.

"Bobby"—and suddenly, my ruminations are reinterrupted—"can you stop being a jerk?"

It's them again.

"I'm a jerk? They're selling pizza in the snack bar. I saw a girl with a slice."

"Can you just forget pizza?"

"Can I just *what*?"

"Can you just . . . Never mind."

His girlfriend speaks in that I'm-so-over-this-asshole voice I know so well.

*Think about the Jews*, I repeat to myself. *Think about the Jews, think about the Jews.*

"Some fucking honeymoon!"

*Think about the Jews!*

"Bobby!"

"Whatever, Marla. These look like fucking pizza ovens. I'm gonna get a slice. You want a slice? I'm getting a slice." He makes a show of shaking his head, all *I'm a long-suffering guy*. But ironic, like the whole routine is some kind of UCB Harold improv setup: *You're at Auschwitz, fighting with your girlfriend, about pizza. Go!*

At least that's what I think till Bobby turns away from the incinerator to start for the door and spots me standing back there. (I'm distorting things; if I were looking at me, old bad-hair Jew in black slouched against the smudgy rear wall of the body-burning facility, I would probably not say "standing," I'd say "skulking." Or, better yet, "lurking." But old-guy posture aside, in my mind I was *this* close to attaining the epic spiritual/empathetic crescendo I was praying for. To totally connect. Until—)

"You see something you like, asshole? I saw you staring at my wife back there. You some kinda freak?"

If I rush him, can I just push Bobby in the oven and lock those doors? I've got the element of surprise. And I have a feeling Marla might not mind. Marla, who I had not really clocked before, has a hard, Joan Jettish face, pretty but no-nonsense, aglow with either righteous anger or rigorous skin care. Despite the Ralph Lauren—make that Lifshitz—sweater tied around her neck, she looks like she might have done some time with the Nazi Low Riders before cleaning up and throwing in with alt-right khaki-

and-polo Bobby. Mr. Nationalist Lite. And yes, Jews will replace you.

(A scrap of paper that survived that day bears a single, scrawled line: *Grandiose sadness at the Six Million.*)

So there it is. I wanted that grandiose emotion.

Maybe that's the real reason I'm so upset by Bobby's pizza-oven comment. Because—mortifying but true—I kind of agree with him. How ungrandiose can you get? I fucking hate myself.

The guy has outed me for my own cheesy brain. He's harshing my Holocaust. *Fuck!*

I mean, you want to meditate on the ovens. But not like that. Now I just want to shove the guy in. All I can think is, *If I lock the door, will he suffocate? Or is there a way to scuttle up and out of the chimney?*

# CHAPTER 11
## *UNWORTHY*

🚌 🚌 🚌

I'D SPENT MONTHS BEFORE MY TRIP poring over books and testimonials, diving into Shoah, consuming as much of the requisite and ennobling literature as I could. Only to arrive and bear witness, not to the vast travesty represented by the camps, but to my own troubling incapacity to comprehend it. Is there a reason our thoughts cannot be as dignified as our intention? Am I the only human who, confronted with the unspeakable, finds a deeper well of the unspeakable in himself, a lightweight, no-class, sporadic descent into that which he can but dimly comprehend—the horror of being wholly unworthy of the horror itself?

"It's all fake anyway," Bobby drones on, "it's a reenactment. Like on *Forensic Files*, where they get actors who can't get work in real show business to do pretend murders. It's reenactment architecture."

Here he launches into the story, made popular by deniers, of the so-called fake chimneys constructed by the Russians in 1947, to give a sense of what the place looked like when it was running on all cylinders, next to the gas chamber.

"That doesn't mean the whole thing is bogus," Marla snaps, "it just means they made improvements."

I'm starting to appreciate this woman. Even if her taste in men is questionable, and she's got a Keane-eyed unicorn on her upper thigh the size of a pie plate. (Speaking of: given how hot it is, bare arms and torsos are all over the place, along with bare legs and what used to be called short-shorts. Not, mind you, that I'm advocating a dress code. If folks want to dress the same way for Auschwitz they would for Space Mountain, who am I to judge? Like Madge and Tad from Texas, in their shameless vacation-wear—matching *It's Beer O'clock Somewhere!* T-shirts—you find your cliché and you stick to it.)

I've worn the same stupid black jeans and black tee since I was fifteen, and it finally seems appropriate.

But where'd we leave off? Putting Bobby in the oven. Right.

If he does suffocate, and I linger, will I take delight in his muffled pleading, the scrape of his fingers on the door? Will that make me Nazi-evil or just evil-evil?

Is it better or worse to kill blindly, for ideology—or because it's a job? Or maybe because of something pettier, like— going out on a limb here—maybe the deceased was an idiot, who made you feel like an idiot for thinking the exact same idiotic thought they did.

Not for the last time I think, *What is wrong with me?* Then wonder if I'm talking out loud.

I had hoped, I admit, that coming here would make me a better person. Instead, I feel like the inside of my brain is sinking into vicious quicksand. Quicksand with piranhas in it, streaming on Twitch.

I play out the Khaki Bob–killing scenario—right to the moment I'm arrested by camp police, if they have them.

(Are they among us now, in plainclothes? Is that amiable mook in the Megadeth top undercover?) Or—I can't stop—what if I make it to the bus, only to be yanked off by the Oświęcim constabulary? Cuffed and perp-walked up the aisle to hisses and whispers—or maybe applause.

*Did you hear? Gerald put a guy from Google in the oven!*

(I don't know why I assume Bobby works for Google. I just know.)

I give the crematorium doors one last look, and split before things get worse. On no level is this a good story; it's just what happened.

Fleeing the happy couple, Bobby and Marla, running on nothing but epigenetic instinct, I speed-walk out to the counting ground, hyper aware of the crunch of gravel under my boot. Gripped by awareness of treading on a mass grave. But where else can you tread? Has all that just happened cheapened the experience? Or was I cheap to begin with? That's one question. The other is, what kind of person makes a death camp about himself? Narcissism on parade. It's the eternal struggle: sunburn on neck versus suffering of millions of innocent human beings.

My first death camp, and I feel like I'm doing it wrong.

Unable to find my comrades, I latch on to another tour group. Follow them to a barracks with the sense that I'm cheating on my group. Some kind of bus tour adulterer. Or at least a traitor.

I listen up as the tour guide, a man so short all I can see is the logo on his Knicks cap in front of his crew—unless he's normal-sized, and they're hoopsters—explains about the barracks, how a thousand people squeezed into a room for two hundred. Recalling how my favorite detective novelist, Philip Kerr, sends his Third Reich dick, Bernie Gunther, to the camps, where the Nazi-hating gumshoe describes the nightmare within a nightmare of being consigned a bottom bunk, under an inmate with typhus. Gunther knows it's typhus because of the dripping, and the stench.

But today there is no stench. Today the site is immaculate. And I realize the obvious: without the stench, without mud, blood, wailing, and death, this isn't hell. This is the Museum of Hell.

Somehow I've left the barracks and wandered downfield to the railroad siding where a lone period boxcar sits on the track. "The selection!" I hear myself cry. I'm standing on the spot where notorious Auschwitz doctor and obsessive twin collector Josef "Beppo" Mengele made his selections while an orchestra of inmate musicians played waltzes nearby.

Survivors recall that Mengele sniffed a flower in his lapel as he decided the fate of new arrivals. Thumb to the right: gas and chimney. To the left: hard labor. Fast, unspeakably horrible death or slow, unspeakably horrible death.

It does not matter how iconic the scene is, that it's been rendered in a thousand movies, described in books and documentaries into numbing cliché. As I said earlier, will probably say again—and still feel like shrieking—when you're actually standing there, on that ground, all preconceived notions about the place are erased. Think De Niro in *The Deer Hunter*: "*This is this.*" Half my time at the camp

I keep my eyes on the ground, like a crack addict scoping crumbs. I don't know what I'm looking for. It's just . . . this earth, this dirt. Where the dead once marched. I bend down, pick up stones, fill my pockets. If there were a pond nearby I'd probably Virginia Woolf it right then and there.

Instead, staggering off, I'm struck by a strange sensation that the eyes of the murdered are staring up from beneath me, neither judging nor complaining. I crash past a clan of red-faced white people sitting on the ground, as if besotted by emotion, or felled by the blazing Polish sun. It turns out they're chanting, though I don't know what. I leave them and head to the long courtyard between infamous Blocks 10 and 11.

From the outside, these two long buildings, facing each other across a well-maintained walkway and courtyard, might be smallish Greenwich Village brownstones. As you approach the far end of the courtyard, however, a sign urges *Quiet* and noise fades. This is the storied Wall of Death, before which the condemned—mostly Polish politicals—were paraded naked from the adjacent "dressing room" and shot in the neck. Fresh bouquets have been placed on the ground. Pebbles in wall cracks. A guide—this one a brisk, solemn Brit of a certain age who speaks in a super-familiar way I can't place, until I realize he sounds like one of the narrators on the Military Channel (now renamed as the Amerian Heroes Channel). Your cable HQ for all-night WWII and Nazi docs. That solemn, no-nonsense cadence. When business was brisk the SS used air pistols to spare the tender ears of the professionals inside the buildings.

Block 10 was experimentation and sterilization. This

is where, among other miscreants, Dr. Mengele busied himself sewing twins together, injecting dwarf children with gangrene, sterilizing legions of inmates by having them sit on radiated benches. "Business as usual," the guide intones, "for the Thousand-Year Reich." His is the pitch-perfect timbre for the grim business at hand.

Block 11 was the torture building. Over the door, a small sign still visible: *BLOK SMIERCI*. Death Block. A rare case of noneuphemistic Nazi-speak. Block 11 was a warren of torture chambers within the open-air torture of the camp itself. Visitors walk down an oppressive, narrow corridor, peering into each specially designed hell hole. Like the suffocation cell: custom-made so occupants slowly used up available oxygen. Some guards would put candles inside for the prisoners—not to illuminate but to suck up the oxygen, speed asphyxiation. For inmates caught trying to escape there were starvation cells, where victims were basically left to die—slowly—with no food and no water. Causing occupants, in the grips of thirst, to drink from their own urine buckets.

One of the Starvation Rooms' most famous occupants was Maximilian Kolbe, a Franciscan priest, whom John Paul beatified in 1971. For good reason. Upon hearing that ten men were to be thrown in a hunger room and starved to death for the crimes of three men who'd tried to escape, Father Kolbe volunteered to replace one of them. Kolbe had heard the man, Franciszek Gajowniczek, pleading with camp commander Höss that he had a wife and children. Whereupon Kolbe—who was in prison for clothing and sheltering three thousand refugees at his monastery—made the deal that sealed his fate. Declaring that he, himself, was already an old man—he was forty-seven—Kolbe volunteered for his own painful death.

Legend has it the priest remained unremittingly cheerful throughout the ordeal, praying and singing constantly, routinely lifting the spirits of the other prisoners. Ironically, he did not die of starvation. When Kommandant Höss decided occupants of the cell were not starving fast enough, he opted to speed things along and give the prisoners lethal injections. And here, according to Catholic lore, Kolbe sealed his saintly status by extending his arm to his murderers, holding it out of the cell for the shot that would kill him.

Since his martyrdom, Father Kolbe's iconic image has often been portrayed in striped prison garb, receiving a hypodermic injection. Resulting in not just canonization, but official title as Patron Saint of Addictions.

And good news! For $9.99 you can order your very own 1-1/8-inch silver-toned Kolbe medallion from Amazon. Though, not so good, on the Amazon coin Saint Max is not shown taking a shot with his sleeve rolled up, he's holding a book and peering sweetly through a pair of round spectacles. Still, the banner above him reads, *Saint Maximilian Kolbe*, and below: *Patron Saint of Addictions*. Which, not to go all grammar fascist, sounds not so much like he's a saint for addicts—a junkie saint!—but that he's the saint for their habits. So that, in effect, addictions have their very own saint, while addicts are left on their own. I'm already feeling sorry for myself.

Truth be told, I am not sure what to think about some old $300-a-day smack jones getting its own holy man, while guys who had the habits—we lowly ex-gutter hypes—must wrestle through life's struggles saintless, on our own. But let's not cry about it. The Lord works in mysterious ways. As I write this now, ogling the Amazon-sold Auschwitz martyr ornament, I've made my peace. But I can't lie. When they start cranking out the Saint Bird medallions, the Saint Lennys and the Saint Art Peppers, I'll be first to violate my own anti-Amazon policy and token up. Whatever it takes, you have to stay on the right side of the Lord.

# CHAPTER 12
## *TRAUMA NOSH*

🚌 🚌 🚌

AFTER THE STARVATION CHAMBER, things do not get any better. I walk down the hall to the next cubicle. This turns out to be the Standing Room. I peer into a three-square-foot box in which prisoners could, literally, do nothing but stand. "Had an apartment like that in college," yucks Tad from Texas, which lets me know I have somehow stumbled back into my own stellar group. Prisoners, we are told, were expected to stand all night, then work a ten-hour day. Then repeat.

A woman in a hijab and her partner move quickly away from Tad, as do what look to be a family of Norwegians—blond, blue-eyed types right out of Hitler's Master Race catalog. The one he probably snuck into the bunker bathroom with him. I follow the Super-Whites out of the hall-way and into a stairwell, where a throng of stunned-looking attendees clomp their way up the stairs. There is a kind of weary shock that settles on the faces of visitors. Few, that I can see, cry; or else they cry at the beginning, only to run out of tears midtour, and emerge with that blown-out, psycho–emotionally drained expression you see everywhere at the camps.

(I'm reminded, touring these chambers, how—back

in America—the National Park Service offers overnights at Alcatraz. Defanging past brutality by rendering it B&B adjacent. From Park Service literature: "At the end of the evening, the group retires to their individual cells in D-Block . . . Each cell has a cot with a covered 4-inch foam mattress . . ." How long, one wonders, until Auschwitz is modified for guests? Or maybe it already is, and it's a VIP thing. For the Zuckerberg set. Death with Internet capability.)

Moving on—

No more cells now. We are facing actual displays of actual items, recovered when the Allies liberated the place. Call it an eloquent frenzy of objects. Mementos behind glass: a mountain of suitcases, countless tangled eyeglasses, discarded artificial limbs. Who assembled these? Were they arranged? Dumped in? (Among their other issues, it would seem, the Nazis had serious hoarding problems.) And then I spot it, the most startling thing I've ever seen: the hair. An unimaginable mass of human hair: nearly two tons, according to the plaque.

Shorn from the newly dead by the Sonderkommandos, Jews whose job, as we know, was to drag the freshly gassed corpses from the chamber, wrench the gold teeth from their mouths, and shave their heads for extra food or cigarettes. Said hair, tainted with Zyklon B, was sent off to be turned into carpets, cloth, or delicate fibers for detonating bombs. The ashes, gathered in heaps, served to fertilize the kommandant's garden; the Germans, apparently, being early recyclers. (Ideas, as George Bernard Shaw tells us, are not responsible for the people who embrace them.)

The kommandant's house, by the way, is lovely, and would not be out of place in Greenwich, Connecticut.

His children loved to have tea parties. You can almost see the little Aryan-ettes on the picnic blanket; pinkies out, sipping pretend oolong. Not everybody knows it, but the Third Reich was a time of tea cakes. According to Elisabeth Kalhammer, Hitler's maid, the man in charge loved midnight cake, lie-ins, and tea from porcelain china cups.

Who would have guessed? Given their master's spartan image, the last thing Goebbels & Co. wanted the public to know was what a layabout Hitler was. In truth, according to Ms. K, "führer cake"—an apple cake strewn with nuts and raisins—had to be baked each day and left out every night. In a 2014 essay about Kalhammer, the *Independent* reported, "[Hitler] was also partial to chocolate biscuits and scones with tea, which he would drink from a Nymphenburg porcelain cup."

And yes, *Nymphenburg* is doing a lot of work in that sentence.

Fast-forward three-quarters of a century, and Hitler would doubtless become just another aging boomer, asprawl on a sofa eating Mickey D's and watching cable all day. Some lazy bastard with unlimited power, racist intent, and generals he calls his own. Oh wait . . .

But forget the long-gone tea sweets. That was then. More disturbo, right now, is that the former kommandant's lushly gardened mansion is not open to the public. Because it is now private property. Somebody lives there. You can almost hear the realtor tiptoeing up to the subject, testing to see if the whole concentration-camp-in-the-backyard thing is a dealbreaker. Or maybe—given the climate of our times—a plus. What really sells the place.

Not that Kommandant Höss had much time to enjoy the real estate. In his crushingly dull memoir, *Death Dealer: The Memoirs of the SS Kommandant at Auschwitz,* the kvetchy sadist complains mightily about the pressure he was under. "Burning 2,000 people took about twenty-four hours in the five stoves. Usually we could manage to cremate only about 1,700 to 1,800. We were thus always behind in our cremating because as you can see it was much easier to exterminate by gas than to cremate, which took so much more time and labor." Whine, whine, whine.

Forget Höss's lovely, state-provided house. Auschwitz itself is arguably sanctified ground. Except, perhaps, for the cafeteria, which I have somehow once again found myself in front of.

Is Auschwitz vegan? Hitler was famously vegetarian—not counting the Bulgarian fecal matter his personal physician, Dr. Morell, would mix in with his morphine and methedrine injections. (Is fecal matter "meat"? The eternal question! However you categorize it, nutritionally speaking, Doc Morell thought it would give his cake-loving patient stamina.) But syringe food doesn't really count as food. Does it?

Hitler had an image to maintain—teetotaler, animal flesh avoider, not . . . junkie. What might he have made of the mysteriously (to me) peckish visitors pouring into the Auschwitz snack bar? Personally, I find myself just standing there, on the modest road out front, staring with some grim amalgam of shock, revulsion, and genuine disbelief. The actual pizza ovens are, on some level, just as disturbing as the ovens in the crematorium. Cemeteries don't usually have snack bars—why are things different when it's land where the dead were murdered as well as buried?

Or is that what generates such rampant appetites? Imagining all that killing and body-disposing?

Sensing my dismay, or more accurately my confusion, an old-school gentleman in a homburg hat and thick tweed suit, no small touch in eighty-plus weather, steps beside me and stares at the death campers shoving pizza and chicken legs into their faces.

Seated around outdoor tables, those paying their respects can top off the experience, or gear up for it, by gorging on hot dogs, ice cream, burgers, the already discussed pizza, and—by way of honoring the nation—a small array of zesty Polish dishes. To name a few of the fast food offerings. There's also a vending machine with coffee outside.

To compare and contrast, prisoners started the day with a half a liter of coffee—really boiled water with grain coffee substitute. According to the Auschwitz-Birkenau State Museum literature, the meal of the day, at noon, was soup: theoretically "with potatoes, rutabaga, and groat, along with rye flower and a food extract called AVO." *AVO?* you're probably asking. *I wonder what that is.* Well, me too! As often happens, with all things Holocaust, one can go down a very dark rabbit hole trying to track the origins of such stuff.

Turns out (am I the only geek who finds this fascinating?) the AVO company was founded in 1921, under the name August Vodegel, which was quickly shortened to—if I may quote the company's own spritely PR—"the memorable brand name AVO." Yes!

Memorable as the name is, however, poring over their website promo, it's clear company historians have some-

how forgotten their flavor contribution to the Third Reich—
that tasty death camp lunch additive.

Still, I'm happy to hear AVO is still around. Now making, among other things, "highly effective additives and
functional ingredients." *Yummo!*

"The customer is our priority," beams AVO's online
brochure. Begging the question, who were the customers
seventy years ago? Doomed slaves slurping up rutabaga
slop, or the SS purchasing agents who bought the filler
from Germany's top purveyor of sausage filler?

Either way, like I say, AVO is still going strong. Having
paid, as far as I can tell, no price for their part in feed-
ing the future dead. And making a profit off it. Why? Because then and now, as the folks at AVO are busting their
buttons to tell you, they remain the "spice specialist with
expertise in both taste and technology." Even when, back
in the bad old days, said technology (I can't stop repeating) was geared to starving human beings deemed unfit to
live by the master-racers who wrote the checks. If I may:
"From the outset, we chose to take our very own path—
even if it is not always the easiest!"

Exactly! Nobody said doing business with Nazis was a
walk in the park—but damn it, AVO did it! And here they
are today, still putting the delish in delicious. Or not.

The food at Auschwitz—and every other camp—is
universally described as revolting. That soup, for example,
was basically just fetid water. So the choice was between
eating and being sick or not eating and being hungry. And
being sick. Throw in the nightly three hundred grams of
black bread for supper, and the average prisoner's nutritional intake came to roughly eight hundred (barely edi-

ble) calories a day. Leaving the same average prisoner so depleted he or she began to consume their own fat, until fully emaciated in a matter of weeks. At which point, too sick to work, they would either expire on their own or require the labor of camp guards to cram into the gas chamber.

Okay, forgive the over-AVOing. Where were we? Oh, right. My silent, tweed-clad old comrade and I stand together by the café and stare for what seems like an eternity.

I imagine I see the faces of the dead and starving staring from just off the patio, in the shade of the Coca-Cola awnings and signs for chicken wings and pizza. And I wonder—wouldn't you?—which is the travesty: the eating or the forgetting? Or are they forgetting? Maybe they are meditating on the dead even as they munch? Why not? Here we are at the Snack Bar of the Damned. (The Six Million? Try the pepperoni! Mengele injected babies with arsenic? Have a Fanta!)

The sin—if I may be so judgmental—is not that the folks here have forgotten the vicious truth. I mean, we are here in memory of it, at this sprawling camp-slash-museum. No, the sin—and maybe it's just me—is that the snackers, by snacking, seem not sufficiently unhappy.

Who knows? Maybe all these people, they're grief-eating. Stuffing their feelings. Like the time I ate twenty-seven Twinkies after my father did the thing in the Oldsmobile with the motor running. But I did that, need I mention, not basking on a death camp patio (three words that sing), but alone, at three a.m., hunkered over a sink. Setting the pattern for a lifetime. Eventually the Twinkies turned to heroin. But that's a whole other book.

Finally, without looking at me, my formal new friend doffs his homburg and begins to speak, in an accent that may be Polish, Czech, Belarussian, or Lithuanian. One of the victimized nations. "You know, it is assumed the visitors' center—the souvenir shop, café, toilets, etc.—was built after the place was reopened for tourism. The truth is, that edifice was constructed in the early forties. This is the very spot where prisoners were tattooed and disinfected, where their heads were shaved. Their traumatic entry into hell. Presently commemorated by tourists feasting upon pizza."

His language is so formal. The look I give him earns me a long-suffering smile. And a shrug. "This"—sounds like *zis*—"is the problem. You have deniers saying that, because of this travesty"—he aims a stern gaze at the café—"the whole thing is some kind of lie. Well, my friend, do not believe that. Nobody is claiming that blood did not run on this very spot. Just that, where it ran, there is now a, what do you call it, a snack bar."

The distinguished gentleman walks away without ever introducing himself, merely stopping, as he goes, to add, "Make inquiries if you like." This with a realpolitik, generations-of-torment shrug. Before he stops again, far enough away so he almost has to shout, though he's so old his voice is weak. "A joke," he calls in my direction. "What did the hog say to the butcher?"

"I give up," I say, and, one more time, he aims the world's most disenchanted grin my way.

"You bring out the wurst in me."

With that, he's gone, back into the crowd. I don't know if he's going in, or coming out. It hits me that he might be a survivor. Or a nonsurvivor. A dybbuk. A shade of Auschwitz. Shunning the afterlife to walk the camp enlightening fools like me. The ones he thinks can hear it. Or need to. Is that too dramatic? Is anything too dramatic in this place? Or have I lost my shit entirely? I only wish I could spell "snack bar" the way he pronounced it. I won't even try. Think Bela Lugosi, with Silesian denture issues.

For minutes afterward, I cannot take my eyes off the cafeteria. Patrons, there is no way around it, are really chowing down. What is it about genocide that gives folks such a hearty appetite? And at what point will some savvy marketer take a page from showbiz joints like the Carnegie Deli, or Canter's in Hollywood, and offer sandwiches named for stars? The Carnegie had the Woody Allen. Canters has the Buck Benny. Why can't Auschwitz claim the Primo Levi Pastrami on Rye? Arbeit Macht Fries! Who, exactly, are the death camp marketeers? Why aren't they on this? It's not like naming a celebrity hoagie would be more disrespectful than what's already on the menu—or the fact that there even is a menu. Why aren't people puking on their shoes, on general principal?

Though I don't want to eat, in the interests of journalistic endeavor I enter the joint and take my place at the end of the line. Hard to say what the appropriate post-tour trauma nosh might be. Beyond the cliché surrealism of a genocide nibble parlor, what hits me first is the porcine nature of the proceedings, the across-the-board porkness on parade. Ham sandwich, pepperoni pizza, even Mexican calzone.

Stay with me. It's an innovative culinary flourish, the Mexi-zone, melding Latino and Italian cuisine. And what better place to march it out? Maybe—I know it's a stretch—the multicultural pizza fold-over might be the perfect slap in the face to the place's former Aryan occupants. What would Himmler think?

On the other hand—no kosher food? Really? Can you have kosher food in a pig-centric establishment? Bad Jew that I am, I don't know the answer.

Whether the pork is insult or insensitivity, it's irrational to think the dead would feel better with bagels and matzoh brei. But maybe? Couldn't the café overlords have thrown in a jar of pickles? Am I being petty, or is anything less respectful to Jews mulling their unspeakable history than a ham sandwich? Are there not bound to be Chasids, Orthodox Jews, and Muslims who cannot abide eating food made with treif and haram in the pantry? Nu?

The disconnect between brutal past and fanny-pack-casual, fast-food-and-gift-shop-postcards present may be too obvious to declare. Still, it's hard not to wonder how Father Kolbe and his cellies in the Starvation Room would react if brought back from the grave and allowed to amble out to Calzone-town.

Then again, *I'm* standing here, so what does that make me? Boycotting pizza hardly makes you Mandela. If I find Homburg Man standing in my hotel room later, I'll know that spirit has passed over to flesh, and the collective sighs of a million innocents may have breathed life into a tweed-clad messenger. That or I've lost my fucking mind, and am now full-on delusional. Either way. Who doesn't appreciate a visit from the astral plane?

# CHAPTER 13
## *AN ANNOYING AND SELF-RIGHTEOUS OGRE*

🚌 🚌 🚌

I HAVE NO APPETITE WHATSOEVER, and return to the bus, only to be confronted by a mob of frustrated visitors, some of whom, apparently, have been standing in the sun since long before my crew even got here. I swerve to avoid a squabble between a ticket holder and a non–ticket holder who, for reasons I can't fathom, turns her wrath my way.

"Did you reserve a ticket?"

"Who me? Well, I think my tour—"

"That's it!" she spits, in a Midwest accent, all riled-up Minnesota Nice. "Your tour! Well, maybe not everybody has a tour. Maybe some of us regular folks just came on our own, because we wanted to see, we wanted to experience this thing."

"Well, jeez," is all my quick wits come up with. As if traveling by bus makes me a pasha. But I can't explain. All I can add is, "I understand."

Before another pair of sunbaked stragglers, a pinkish-white couple holding hands in matching pith helmets, interrupt to ask, "Is this the right line for ticket holders?"

The exact gasoline to throw on the fire—how did they know?

"You have tickets?" Miss Minnesota turns to her long-suffering husband and her two want-to-be-swallowed-up-by-gravel preteen kids, then turns back and mad-dogs the papers in Mr. Pith Helmet's hand. For an instant I think Mom is going to snatch them, then drag her family to the front of the line and just elbow their way in. I'm reminded, suddenly, of a time when I was twelve, and my father and I were in Syracuse visiting my sister in college. For some reason the old man decided we should take in a football game. Something we never did. But while we were standing there outside the stadium, a hooded figure came springing up out of nowhere and, in a blur, snatched the tickets from his hands and took off, my squat, out-of-shape father running behind him, screaming, "Thief! Thief!" As if it were the magic word that would startle everyone on hand into action, to stop the lawbreaker. Instead, about forty minutes later, after we'd been ignored by everyone, laughed at by a large blond security cop, my dad somehow talked and complained his way into the stadium, where we made our way down the rows until we stood in front of a smirking older couple, both hale and hearty, and trained in the art of acting innocent. My father pleaded, with greater and greater impotence (can you have *great* impotence?), at the ticket-holding fans, "These seats are mine!" But (of course) they steadfastly ignored him.

Finally, the people behind us told my father to move. And he did.

Memories! Despite his best efforts, my poor little father could not get the "authorities," the stadium security, to give a shit. From that day on, the image of Dad, already a short man, walking back after the chase, seemingly even shorter than when he'd taken off, with fervor, after the evildoers, defined his entire being. Right up to the day he died. Diminished.

An hour later, back at the hotel, the old man said, "That's just the goddamn world." He was an immigrant, and he believed in America. But on the ground it was a sham. In went the knife to my preteen heart. Whatever trace of frustration or rage he might have had just seemed to disappear. Replaced by—what? I'm still not sure.

My father, himself, made it out of Lithuania at ten, eight years after his father was killed in a pogrom. Eight years he had to stay with strangers while his mother, my Russian grandmother, took passage to come and care for a distant older cousin, a grocer in a Pennsylvania coal town, who wouldn't pay for his stepson's travel. She saved up her nickels to book passage for my left-behind father on a boat alone when he was ten. My whole life, I felt nameless guilt that I had it so easy and my father had had it so hard. All he would say, if asked about those missing years, were eight words: "We were the only family without a cow."

Crowded and miserable and morally mortifying as the Auschwitz parking lot seems to be, as I stand here breathing bus exhaust, craning my eyes for a Globule sign, it still seems infinitely preferable to the scene I left back in America. Who hasn't, I tell myself grimly, blown a marriage or three? On the plus side, in my case there was no ambiguity: everything was pretty much my fault.

In our last fight, my soon-to-be-legally-divorced partner called me (stop me if I've told you this one) a "whore." And not without reason. Though I was, even at the screams-in-the-face height of things, taken aback at the use of the word. A whore. No reason the term should be relegated to one gender over the other. (Look at me, breaking down walls!) In any sense, I deserved it. The woman was furious at what she'd found on my computer, evidence of all the usual dickish crap-husband behavior.

Since the whole you're-a-whore exchange, communication with my erstwhile better half had been remarkably friendly. Testament, I suppose, to an uncomplaining worldliness—her own father bailed when she was born, so she'd known how life could fuck you long before I showed up. A big-hearted person I did not deserve, and was lucky to know.

And so, from the perspective of Satan's bus stop in Oświęcim, it's a weird and substantial blessing to have a collapsing life, back in the States, providing counterweight to the crush of history here in fun and sunny Poland. Separation, pre–actual divorce, is proving to be every bit as, oh, let's just say, smooth and non–soul destroying as, by the end, living together had become the opposite. And yes, I will be submitting that last sentence for the Prose That Reads Like a Bowling Ball Bouncing Down the Stairs Award later this year, when application season opens. So many writers go for clarity, erudition, the proverbial lapidary prose. Me, well, I'm going for more of a translated-from-Urdu feel. You either have it or you don't.

Someday I would like to find out how many people's marriages have been burst, like giant fistula, by the sudden prick of e-mail discovery. You can't complain about snooping if somebody finds something, right? None of that *Law & Order* fruit-of-the-poison-tree stuff when it comes to filthy e-mails. Did Al Gore dimly comprehend, when he invented the Internet, its de facto superpower as bad relationship detector? Much as I may have wanted, in my heart, only the best for my ex, when she was still my pre-ex, my actions (cyber and otherwise) told a different story. And now that the marriage is done, I want nothing more than to pay whatever I can afford, or can't afford, to at least try to make things right, to help set her up with our daughter in a new, non-married-to-me life.

And no, I think, staring off from this parking lot to the crematorium chimneys, it's not like owning yourself as an ogre in advance makes you any less of one. It just makes you an annoying and self-righteous ogre.

Suddenly my phone vibrates. I pick up, and hear my little girl. "Daddy?" One word and the accretion of dog-chasing-its-tail miseries, global and private, are simply obliterated.

"Daddy?" That quiver in the voice that could break your heart.

"Hey, Supergirl, what's going on?"

"I got a bear and a racoon and a furry shark."

"Really? Do they like each other? The bear's not biting the shark or anything, is she?" *She*, always. Like it's going to teach her girls can be anything they want, me making the creatures in her stuffy menagerie female. (My first daughter, twenty-three years older, has on occasion viewed my track record with women as evidence of some treachery toward them. I don't agree, but respect her opinion, and find myself bending over backward with her little sister, in no doubt meaningless ways, to compensate. Just in case. The good news is, Daughter One, a politically active feminist—among other things—actually speaks to me. And is there wickedly funny.)

"Dad-dy!" comes my little one's response. And is there anything better than that delighted my-dad's-kind-of-dumbo tone in her voice? "They like each other."

"Just checking," I say "That sounds fun. So what else is going on, baby?"

"Nothin'. We're staying at Grandma's. But her fin is kind of hanging off."

"Grandma's?"

More delighted exasperation. For an instant Auschwitz disappears. "No, silly, the shark."

"It's a grandma shark?"

"Daddy, you're being a nutball!"

*That's my job,* I think but don't say. Keep things nutty, keep life fun, no matter what else is going on. Smile, if you'd like to sing along, when your heart is breaking, for as long as possible.

Does every parent know the bifurcated reality of falling to pieces, and keeping it together, at the same time? For their child? Because, really, when your own parents were screamers and suiciders, insulters and head-through-the-plaster types, you don't want to go that route. (Her big sister got Junkie Daddy; she gets Older Daddy.) And relax, I offer no insights on child-rearing. I wouldn't presume. Except, as a personal credo, to try to screw them up the exact opposite of how you were screwed up when you were their age. I can't quote much poetry, but I can quote Philip Larkin's most famous:

*They fuck you up, your mum and dad.*

*They may not mean to, but they do.*
*They fill you with the faults they had*
*And add some extra, just for you.*

Is it too much to ask the cosmos to not let you fuck up a child that you are responsible for?

Even if you're separated by half a world from the little one you're talking to, they sense everything. They know, even if they don't know they do. Like tiny, two-legged nuance detectors. If, say, you're dripping with self-hate, but trying with all the strength in your tainted soul to cover up, some neuro-tendrils they don't have names for will absorb it; will be, God forbid, mutated by it. And then it's too late. You've been Larkined.

This is the new pattern with my little girl: me asking endless questions because conversation with a three-year-old can be more arduous than Paris climate talks. If more fun. But silence, on the phone, is just unendurable.

How quickly, I wonder, for no more than the thousandth time, did the complexities of guilt, betrayal, and all the rest of life's inherent torments just dissipate for Auschwitz inmates in the face of their new reality: never-ending pain, humiliation, and imminent death? And for the thousand-and-first time, I know that it would be presumptuous, in all the most hideous ways, to even pretend to know the answer.

# CHAPTER 14
## *RESTAURANT HANGMAN*

🚌 🚌 🚌

WHAT COULD BE BETTER, the day after Auschwitz, than a repast at Dresden's famed Am Pulverton restaurant, an establishment that offers the experience of chowing down at a medieval military stockade.

The whole evening for me is like being trapped in Frederick the Great's rec room. Mounted eighteenth-century weapons cram every inch of wall space. It's all I can do not to grab a Potzdam musket and try to blast my way out of paying for the sizzled pork fat, or whatever the hot blob on my plate is called in German. I am, I won't lie, a tad nostalgic at the flintlock pistol hanging beside two once-innovative Jäger rifles, complete with six-inch butt trap for storing greased linen to keep that baby clean. Not to mention, if I may overshare, the nipple safety covering the percussion cap to stave off accidental discharge. (The latter I found out about from my beloved bipolar uncle, who, along with bouts of crippling Sinatra delusion—in his mind he was singing and swinging in Tahoe, instead of suffering in suburban Pittsburgh— collected books on Prussian weapons. Sundays, when I found myself in his charge, I got manic lectures and demonstrations on proper care and handling. None of which I shared with fellow diners. No one likes a show-off.)

To complete the package, the restaurant features "traditional" Teutonic waitresses (can you spell *lacy dirndl*?)—the whole wake-up-and-smell-Franconia package. (When I close my eyes I seem to recall a taxidermy fox, staring like it knew me, but that may not be accurate. I was still not sleeping, and reality, tenuous to begin with, was growing even more quivery. There was also a wolf head, which appeared to wink and whisper insults. I have no idea why it hated me; it was dead when I got there.)

Turns out Frederick (you can learn a lot from a wall plaque) had assembled a great Prussian army, bringing battlefield glory to his nation, a feat so impressive and inspirational that Hitler did not just try and reenact it, he moved Frederick's coffin—as one does—so he could be closer to his dead but kindred spirit. (On that note, I recall talk, during the Trump reign, of digging up Andrew Jackson, replanting him near Mar-a-Lago, with a buffet and twenty-one-gun salute, but then COVID hit, and good times just went away.) Frederick the Great favored those flintlock muskets, and even had one named after him. (On the Trump tip, again, rumor has it, our reluctantly former president's effort to persuade the Colt .45 folks—owned by Cannae Holdings in Hartford—to rebrand their big seller the Trump 45, after his presidential number, was sidetracked when aides pointed out the name was more associated with malt liquor. Causing teetotaler Trump to demur.)

Along with Frederick, we learn, another reigning spirit of Am Pulverton is Augustus the Strong. Who, if I've got this right, multitasked as King of Poland and Grand Duke of Lithuania. In his portrait, along with a super–New York

Dollish ermine coat, Augustus sports the Order of the White Eagle—the same colors (there are no coincidences) my Polish nemeses, the Auschwitz-adjacent McDonald's gang, were showing.

Am Pulverton's menu boasts some seriously distinctive prose. If not entirely coherent, it's still worth repeating. Here goes: "An extraordinary experience and nothing for the faint of heart promises the hangman's meal at the rack or in the arrest. Between all sorts of scary stories we serve you here your last meal—at least for the evening . . ."

Not sure what the management is going for here. And, admittedly, it's a bit obsessive, lasering in on every line on their menu. But after a visit to Auschwitz you find yourself looking for evidence everywhere. Though evidence of *what* is vague, after Auschwitz the search itself needs no explanation. In any event, nothing says dinnertime fun like pretending you're about to be hanged by Germans. Good times!

Who wouldn't want a pig's knuckle the size of Hellboy's fist, or the ever-popular "home-made aspic of suckling pig with tartar and fried potatoes" after that? The menu says, "13,90 euros—already included." Whether what's included is that aspic, or the noose, is never made clear.

Farther down on the menu, families with kids are offered an even cooler option: "Children's birthday parties with a visit of the executioner!" Who says Germans don't have a sense of humor?

Why doesn't America have birthday clowns who pretend to hang children? In twelve-step culture, there's the dictum: "We neither reject the past nor close the door on it." The Dresden restaurant seems to be going for Door

Number Three: reenacting racial murder as rollicking dinner meme. Sort of like telling ghost stories about the Hook in Cub Scout sleepaway camp, if the Hook happened to be your great-grandfather, and he shoved the blade into babies. The whole thing creeps me out, and I say so.

"You shouldn't get so worked up," Shlomo replies. By the grease on his face it's plain he's enjoying the Dresden vittles. Until, out of nowhere, he reveals that he's still getting over Poland.

I'm immediately transfixed. "How so?"

"I haven't been back since I was a little guy," he explains, "headed to a DP camp. I got lucky. Like I told you, I came to America after Truman signed the Displaced Persons Act." Here his eyes mist and he raises them to the ceiling. "June 25, 1948."

Like my own father, who came from Lithuania to America on his own at the age of ten, Shlomo says virtually nothing about the journey. (My old man, when asked, would reply tersely: "Stewed tomatoes." Apparently that was all they fed him on the boat, and he could barely say the words withing getting queasy. Even as a kid, I knew enough not to press him.)

Shlomo, it seems, is similarly affected. It's as if my eighty-year-old friend had to wait until he could get out of Poland, again, before he could even talk about the place. He confides this to Doug, Tito, and me, who happen to be holding down the non-singing end of the table. Did I mention the German sing-along? Don't ask. Doug, it appears, is still semi-traumatized from nearly being swept into a conga line in Warsaw. "I like participation," he says, "I just don't like *forced* participation." Amen!

The fact that Shlomo is such a sweet guy—if I may generalize and stereotype—makes our political squabbles that much more disconcerting.

Case in point: After hangman meat, we steer back into our regular ongoing conversation. Sylvan "Shlomo" Melman, see, is a breed of old-school Jew I have not encountered, very much in league with evangelists. My first born-again alter kocker.

"What you have to understand," he says, after our Frederick the Great plates have been cleared, "is that the Bible predicted Hitler. It's right there: Book of Esther 3:13 tells of an enemy that wants the destruction of the Jews. And the letters were sent by post. *Destroy all Jews! Kill every last one . . . and take their spoils.* It's right there in the King James."

But where my friend gets more adamant, downright serious, is on the subject of Donald Trump and King Cyrus. Worked up by the subject, Shlomo's doing his pants-hitching thing, reaching down and yanking them north, so the belt rests comfortably under his gentle man-breasts. And yes, by now, here in 2022, all things Trump off-gas a quaint and musty smell. I hope because he's long gone. But the story's worth telling, I think, because it's not about Donald—it's about Shlomo.

That's why I'm sharing. Because there's something about this older gentleman in creased high-rise blue jeans and tucked-in button-down shirt. Shlomo's got a neat, no-nonsense, old-guy style. (And yes, I may as well say it: I'm always looking for role models. I imagine, when you're ninety-one, finding a ninety-nine-year-old who doesn't drool must feel like its own triumph of the will.)

The minute the Persian king hopped on the throne in Babylon, Shlomo declares, he issued a decree authorizing the Jewish people to return home and attend to the temple. The clincher, for Shlomo, is a beauty: "Cyrus was a schmuck. A real pistol. Loudmouth. Not any kind of holy guy. But he did good things for our people." (And this is before Trump took the reins and moved the capital of Israel to Jerusalem.) "Like the evangelists say, the man is profane. He's a cheater. He sins, but I'll say it again, he's great for the Jews! He's predicted, my friend."

"He may be," I say. "What I don't get is why God would think the best idea was to make their modern savior a racist, anti-Semitic sleazeball who ran beauty pageants so he could drill peepholes in the dressing room and perv on naked teens."

"He's not anti-Semitic."

"Oh, so the other stuff is true?"

Cue meshuggener shrug. "So he's a rascal. But he doesn't have to *not* be. He doesn't even have to believe. He's not a preacher. He's a doer."

"A doer?"

"He does things. Good, good things!"

After a few days, Shlomo and I have it down to a science. Any time there's a lull in the tour, Shlomo pipes up and tries to convert me. (Ironic, since we're both Jewish.) We generally find ourselves on the same floor, so if it's not over dinner, like now, it's while we wait for the elevator down to breakfast, or while we're *on* the elevator.

"I know you hate me for what I believe," Shlomo will challenge, between floor five and lobby.

"I do not!" I'll reply, as the gleaming elevator doors part.

Or waiting for coffee and dessert, at night. "You hate me." Slurp, dunk, slurp.

"I do not." Dunk, slurp. Repeat.

"It's okay. Israel needs a friend."

"Shlomo . . ."

"I know." Helpless shrug. "You hate me."

"I don't hate you."

"You do. I'm a Republican. Okay. But you know what I say? Republican Shmublican. Where's the puzzle? Obama is a crypto-Muslim."

"Come on, you're an intelligent man."

"Thank you. My friend, the big-shot writer."

"That's so not true."

"I'd like to write. You know, I have a story."

"Of course. Does it involve Trump secretly being Jesus?"

"Your father was a refugee, right? I bet he was very patriotic."

"He was."

"And he loved the Jews?"

"I guess so."

"Then I bet he knew all about Esther 9:5–14. That's the story I want to write. How the Jews struck down all their enemies with the sword, killing and destroying them, and they did what they pleased to those who hated them. Esther had the king impale the ten sons of Haman."

"That seems a little harsh."

"Oh, a funny boy. A regular Red Buttons over here."

But this time, in the middle of the Right-Wing Enlightenment Hour, Shlomo sighs, and when I ask what's the matter, he tells me—"I'm sorry, it's my wife."

"You talked to her?"

"This afternoon. But I got the time wrong and interrupted *Ankur's Treasure Chest*."

"Come again?"

"*Ankur's Treasure Chest*, on one of those shopping channels. She watches religiously. I let her buy things, then I cancel them before the order goes through. The people at Shop LC are great about it. They know. They get old people all the time. People on drugs; lonely people who just want to talk to the operator. With me over here, I guess she's all three."

"You don't ever let her keep anything?"

"There's a necklace. Her birthstone. I let that arrive, about five years ago. That one she loves. That one she kept. And now I just wrap it up. Put stamps on the package every once in a while and let her find it again. You know, with the dementia . . ."

"I understand," I say.

I suppose there are better definitions of love. But right now I can't think of any.

Shlomo looks away, maybe dries a tear and sniffles, blows the eau de Dresden out of his not-diminutive nose. "You can't understand. We've been married fifty-three years. After she tears the paper off, I let her show it to me. I mean, you should see how excited she gets."

Nights he gives her the necklace, he tells me, she dresses up a little.

"Then I step behind, both of us in front of the bathroom mirror, and I swear, the look in her eyes, I don't know. To me, she's there. The doctors say the light's on, nobody driving the subway . . . But, well, what does it matter? Happy is happy."

Shlomo smiles, and call me sentimental, I hope that Greta Melman, in another country, can feel it. And that the whole colon thing isn't slowing her down. I could tear myself up thinking about old Shlomo in his apartment. There he is, up late, pulling out the tape and wrapping paper, making the tissue paper just so, all so the woman he loves can be surprised one more time. A story I could not have heard, I remind myself, without getting on the bus.

Everyone, it would seem, packs their own pretour sadnesses.

# CHAPTER 15
## *MUNICH*

🚌 🚌 🚌

BEFORE WE MAKE THE TREK TO BUCHENWALD, concentration camp number two on the itinerary, we're scheduled to get a taste of its closest big city, Munich. But not just normal Munich. Munich during Oktoberfest. Happy days!

For non–Nazi compulsives, Munich is where young Hitler started off as a beerhall table-banger and budding demagogue. And here on the ground, breathing beer hall fumes, it seems plausible it can happen again. Maybe in the next five minutes. I'd had, you see, the peculiar thrill of getting lost during this hell-party at dusk, while a bunch of drunk-on-their-ass Hermann Göring lookalikes in tight leather short-shorts and feathered dunce caps blocked the street to break into what I could only assume was the Nazi equivalent of the can-can. Makes sense that Hitler got his start where beer-shitting your lederhosen is a badge of honor. In one bad moment I found myself cornered in an alley and thought, *This is how it ends!* Mauled to death by a bunch of gone-to-fat *Sound of Music* goons in soiled hot pants, so close I could smell their Löwenbräu burps. Were they really hissing "Juden," or was I imagining it? I tried to get pictures but couldn't stop moving, so they came out blurry.

Earlier in the afternoon, we passed the site of the Bürgerbräukeller—the legendary bierhalle from which Hitler staged his Beer Hall Putsch in November 1923. And yes, it is difficult not to see that first umlaut in Bürger-bräukeller as a pair of hanging Hitler balls over the open mouth of Germany. Legend has it, however, that Hitler was a uni-ball, and I don't know if there are actual uni- or semi-umlauts, or what they would be used for. Speculation about Hitler's junk—there is the whole "micro-penis" thing (don't google), plus rumors of Deep Trench man-on-man love in World War I—runs through underground Nazi lore and literature. Though I guess we'll never know about the half-an-umlaut.

With the notable exception of John Dillinger, by no stretch a political criminal, the schvantzes of above-the-fold society-threatening monsters have not notably been curated. Unless they have, and we don't know, and there's some fascist fanboy who likes to doff a swastika jock, slap on some Wagner, and march by the humidor where he keeps the führer's zuckerstange (yes, some Germans call their penis a "candy cane"), beside his Mussolini merkin. Il Duce was rumored to shave, so his *ari del vostri capelle* could glisten as smoothly as his skull. But we have no photos, unless there are a few, framed and autographed, kept safe in a special place beside said fanboy's (or fangirl's) Axis cock-locker. I guess we'll never know.

Of course, getting arrested after firing a bullet in the bürgerhalle ceiling and failing to take over Bavaria—first step in toppling Weimar—turned out to be a great career move for young Adolf. Fortified by hollow leg-sized steins of Münchner Weisse, Hitler's band of loyalists surrounded the beer hall, then hit the streets we're bussing through now toward the Ministry of Defense, only to be stopped by state police officers. Gunshots were exchanged. Four police officers and sixteen Nazis ended up dead. The soon-to-be party leader got knocked to the pavement and suffered a dislocated shoulder before—according to contemporaries—crawling on hands and knees in the gutter until he was rescued and whisked away in a waiting Mercedes.

To commemorate the Beer Hall Putsch, the National Socialists returned to the scene of the uprising, in front of the burgerhalle, every year on the anniversary. Until the Thousand-Year Reich collapsed twelve years later. (And quick question to you, good men and women who designed Microsoft Word's "spelling and grammar" tool, why exactly should "reich" automatically be capitalized to "Reich"? What's the thinking here?)

Suzannah tells us the whole story (with far more drama) as we roll by the site of the beer hall where it happened. Now, unless I misheard, the home of an Apple Store. Of course. We get a bit more history, familiar to anyone with even passing knowledge of the Hitlerian origin story. And learn how, comfortably ensconced in Landsberg, a curiously accommodating prison, the budding scourge of the free world was allowed to loll around jotting down his thoughts and entertaining guests.

"Hitler penned *Mein Kampf* in prison," Suzannah continues, "and it went on to became an instant best seller, with more than twelve million copies printed."

"Probably the only best seller," I pipe up, "with fourteen pages devoted exclusively to syphilis!"

My interruption results in thunderous silence from my fellow riders, and an audible sigh from our leader. Suzannah aims what can only be described as a look of weary concern my way. Her glare, I suspect, as much from annoyance at my unasked-for contribution as the suspicion it would be the first of many.

Trying to redeem myself, I decide to double down, really impress the woman with my erudition. "He called it the Jewish problem," I said.

To which Suzannah, from her tour-guide perch a mere foot or three from my seat, replies in a voice so low only I can hear, "I hope you're not going to be *my* Jewish problem."

No one hears this but me and Josef, the driver, and he betrays no more than a sly quarter-smile I happen to catch in the rearview. At this moment, I know I kind of love the woman.

Not missing a proverbial beat, Suzannah goes on to explain how German law forbade any republication or redistribution of the original book, how you have to comb through antique stores to find it. All this, of course, before Germany's Institute for Contemporary History swooped in after the copyright lapsed in December 2015, to republish the Nazi bible to enormous success. The head of the institute told CNN he was "quite surprised" that public interest was so strong in Germany. Because, really, who'd have guessed *Mein Kampf* would sell 85,000 copies the year of its rerelease? (On the other hand, back in the day, even the *New York Times* had nice things to say about it. One James Gerard, in a review published on October 15, 1933, praised the author for "his unification of the Germans, his destruction of communism, his training of the young, his creation of a Spartan State animated by patriotism, his curbing of parliamentary government, so unsuited to the German character; his protection of the right of private property are all good . . ." You get the picture. Pretty much a big *NYT* hats off to Hitler.) Whatever. It's not like there's a resurgence in neo-Nazi activism, or that members of the AfD, Germany's ultra–right wing party, are going around spraying swastikas on synagogues, or taking Nazi-salute selfies at memorial sites. Come on, man!

The grim truth of the matter: some memorial sites have introduced an "extremist clause," prohibiting access to anyone wearing clothes that refer to the Third Reich. So fair warning, when you're heading off to a genocide site, keep the Himmler-wear in the drawer if you want to get through the gate. At Buchenwald, where we're headed, the number of reported anti-Semitic incidents has doubled since 2015.

But back to *Mein Kampf*. (I know, I can't let it go.) For a fun five minutes, check out Amazon's capsule description, which tells how the book details Hitler's childhood, the "betrayal" of Germany in World War I, the desire for revenge against France, the need for lebensraum (living space) for the German people, the glorification of the "Aryan" race, and the means by which the Nazi party can gain power—which the author identified as the extermination of international poisoners, "a thinly veiled reference to Jews."

Thinly veiled! Exactly the words any sane person would use to describe *Mein Kampf*. Oh, that subtle Hitler! Give it up to Amazon for keeping the Jew-hate on the downlow. Here in the Proud Boys and 3 Percenter era, the English version has been selling like hotcakes. But really, Hitler's prose just sings in any language.

The final high point of our Munich day is a visit to Hofbräuhaus, a football-sized beer hall dear to Nazis everywhere. Here, according to legend, Hitler and the National Socialists held their premier meeting. Among the faithful, Hitler's virgin oratorical effort is known as the Why We Are Anti-Semites speech, a full-throated denunciation of Jews and those who love them.

Fast-forward seventy years and, if the place is full of Nazis, they're doing an admirable job of fronting like Regular Volk. Boisterous patrons sit at ridiculously long tables, beneath chandeliers that look big enough to hide a family of five. The lights hang from high-vaulted ceilings painted with scenes of rustic German life. Most of the overhead scenes appear to involve agriculture, though I'm sure, if you squint hard enough, you might find a warm tableau of rustic Jew-beating.

Diners and drinkers enjoy their fare in what the brochures describe as "homestyle," meaning people you don't know enjoy the fun of sipping their liters of beer with people they don't know. All to the relentless blast of the oompah-oompah band on hand to keep things authentic. Along with its football-field dimensions, Hofbräuhaus boasts one of the largest array of beers in the city. Not one of which do I feel qualified to describe. *Perky, yet gently belch-inducing, with a hint of man-froth . . .* No.

Being a teetotaler, like the führer himself, I don't even want to go in. Instead, while the rest of the team bonds over brew, I dawdle up and down the streets, skulking around corners to check the less touristy nooks and crannies. Most fascinating, for reasons I can't explain, are the butcher windows. Again and again, I'm struck by the pigs dangling by their hind feet, upside down, as if doing headstands in some porcine yoga studio. ("Like SS victims of old," I hear, from a voice just behind me. But if I tell you it's Homburg Man, come from Auschwitz to dog and enlighten me, I'm not sure you'd believe me. Or if you should. I'm not sure *I* believe me. And yet . . .)

No doubt there are metaphors aplenty in the chains of hearty sausage slung up, down, and over all the other fresh-from-the-slaughterhouse meat goods. Don't come to Germany if you don't want to see how the sausage is made. Germany is a sausage factory. Before I can dive into that, Douglas comes screaming across the street, hands flapping in front of him, and throws his arms around me.

"Oh Gerald, thank God!"

Poor Doug is panting so hard it takes a minute for him to get the words out. Or wait, he's not panting. He's crying.

Uh-oh.

"Douglas, what happened?"

"It's . . . It's . . . T-T-Tito," he manages, after unballing a tissue and blowing his nose. "He's g-g-g-gone."

"What do you mean, *gone*?" Since we're talking sausage, I have seen the way his partner chowed down breakfast links, and wonder if they've finally killed him.

But it's not that. "I think," Douglas cries, "somebody s-s-s-snatched him."

"What? I know Tito's Latino, but I had no idea they have ICE in Bavaria."

"I don't mean s-s-snatched," he sputters on, after I peel him off me. "I mean . . . I-I-I don't know what I mean. I'm not good in a crisis. Oh, he's just d-d-d-disappeared." More tears.

When I finally manage to calm him down—resentfully, I'm ashamed to admit, since I really want a pic of that inverted SS yoga pig, but now feel like I can't stop to snap it—Douglas tells me they were at the Hofbräuhaus, sharing a stein, when Douglas got up to visit the men's room. "In a few minutes I come back, and . . . and he's just G-G-G-GONE! Like that young girl in *Taken*!"

"*Taken*?"

"The Liam Neeson movie. Where his daughter is stolen and sold!"

"I know the movie," I respond, without saying the obvious. There probably aren't a lot of princes and billionaires out there buying senior citizens at secret sex-slave auctions. Then again, seventy or not, Tito is one handsome man. Why his partner thinks I've got the Liam Neeson–like Special Forces skills to infiltrate the netherworld of septuagenarian sex profiteers, and snatch him back, I have no idea.

Douglas alternately sobs and chatters as we make our way across the street and around the corner back to Hofbräuhaus. I don't know if I've mentioned, but Douglas is tiny, with a shock of white hair in a pompadour that might top him off at five-four (same height as Stalin) if he stands on his toes. And the whole time we're moving, he's holding onto me, clutching hard, walking unsteadily. Worse, every few steps, my frantic companion kind of hurls himself outward, like he wants to throw himself in front of traffic, and I have to hold him close, though he continues to thrash out with his arms and legs, making sudden, high-pitched screams. I worry, vaguely, that maybe it does look like I'm absconding with the man, whisking him off like some kind of vicious elder-trafficker. Needless to say, a few heads are turning, and I wonder vaguely what the penalty is for Golden Age queen-napping.

Before we step into the cavernous beer hall, I have to stop, pin Doug's arms to his sides, and ask him to calm down. It's a dramatic entrance. The second we're over the threshold, Douglas tears free and runs to one of the long tables on the right. He grabs a left-behind fedora like it's Rosebud and sniffs it, then clutches it to his chest.

"Oh Tito," he wails, "Oh Ti-t-t-to, where are you?"

"Let's retrace our steps," I suggest, just to say something. By now we've got an audience. "So you went to the bathroom . . . ?"

"Yeah, alone," he snaps, suddenly turning on me. "What do you think, I need him to hold my old w-w-w-eenie?"

At this, a family of what, I pray, are exclusively Swedish-speaking blondes gives us a glance, and I hustle him off before they can mace me.

The search continues, and ten tables down we run into Patsy, plainly deep into the Bavarian suds. She learns what has happened and throws her arms around Douglas with such force I worry he's going to be smothered between her ample breasts. Surprisingly (or not), this seems to calm him. Until, going manic all over again, he breaks free, shaking loose and flapping his hands even faster than before.

Without even speaking, as if we've rehearsed, Patsy

and I each take an arm and half guide, half lift our little friend off the floor and carry him through the restaurant, ducking into every stairway, cul de sac, and side room we can find. With no luck.

By now it's ten minutes to four—when the bus is supposed to pick us up in front of the opera house. (At least I think it's an opera house; lowbrow that I am, nine-tenths of the buildings in Olde Munich look like opera houses.)

"Honey, it's okay," Patsy says, barely slowing down when she leans right and projectile vomits over her shoulder, into a trash can. It happens so fast, I only know it happened at all by the modest blob on my left shoe. We are now deep into no-good-deed territory.

"Did you try calling him?" I ask, to at least sound proactive.

Again, Douglas answers with scalding impatience: "Of course I called! But it doesn't matter. Since the big dummy never has his phone with him."

"Are you sure?" Patsy presses.

"Of course I'm sure!" he barks at her, and proceeds to pull out a flip phone and speed dial a number with his left thumb, then hold up a matching phone with his right, so we can watch it ring. "See? I have to carry his, 'cause he's always dropping it." With that, he raises the android to his nose, sniffing and making a face before explaining, "The last time, in M-m-montreal, it fell in a bowl of onion bisque. And it still reeks."

Four minutes to four. We all know the code of the tour: the bus waits for no one. And the reality that Tito might actually be lost makes the last leg of the saga particularly grim. The thought stamps rank panic on Douglas's face.

By the time we make it to the bus, with one minute to spare, Douglas is limp as a pompadoured rag doll between Patsy and me. Patsy upchucks again, straight into a bin. The woman's a pro! That's when it hits me—dummkopf!—the reason more people aren't staring at us is that it's Oktoberfest, when everyone is used to watching too-wasted-to-walk types being dragged out of beer halls and helped through the streets. No one turns a head at Patsy's puking, either. All part of the fun!

Naturally—I won't keep you in suspense—when we step onto the idling bus, Tito is sitting there, placid as a clam. Spotting him, Douglas breaks free from Patsy and me. But instead of running up the aisle and launching into some apoplectic rant, he sits down calmly, composed, with no hint he'd just dragged Four Shot and me seven blocks in a shrieking heap. Douglas quietly asks his partner if he had a nice time. No mention of the tsuris he'd just caused us. No hint that he'd been worried enough to weep in public.

I watch Douglas raise a tiny hand and move a rogue lock of his partner's bottle-black hair back in place, then put Tito's fedora back on his head.

I don't know if I'm angry, touched, or mildly resentful, but before I can decide, Douglas himself turns around, meets my eyes, and mouths a silent *Thank you!*

I mouth back, *No problem.*

Josef puts the bus in gear, and I chalk it all up to the adventure of life on the road.

# CHAPTER 16
## BEAR PIT

🚌 🚌 🚌

BUT BACK TO BUSINESS. Tomorrow begins the trek to Buchenwald. I spend the night writing and sending off draft twenty-nine of the soul-scraping *OG Dad* treatment. Yet again, trying to rework the messy, domestic semi-fuckup of a life to something palatable enough for the network swells who paid good money for it.

Not, as mentioned, that I'm actually writing a script or anything; this is all about nailing down the idea, creating a pitch, so that we can go on to the next step of bleeding out an actual pilot, so they can give me more notes, and then pass on that. Not to complain. There is nothing more revolting than some Audi-leasing calf-implanted pencil-jockey whining about "development hell." My worst day cranking out snappy patter for soup-spitting Jack Klugman is still better than my best day slinging fries at Mc-Donald's. (He said defensively.)

When I'd suggested to Sensitive Exec, on a late-night FaceTime, that we change things up and make the show about a guy hired to write a show about his life as happily married older dad with smart and pretty young wife and little girl he loves, *after* his marriage falls apart and said smart, pretty wife takes the child and dogs and flees the state—"leaving Jerry desolate and alone, but still having to write the happy version of his now-unhappy life"—the visibly uncomfortable Sensitive Exec took a long time before replying. When he finally spoke, it was with the kind of voice you use to ask a pantsless man on the subway who stands too close when he asks for money to please move away. "Uh, not sure I'm feeling that . . ."

"Of course, of course," I burbled. "It was just an idea."

I hung up, feeling completely mortified, and realized I'd been clutching my testicles and pacing. (This was pre-Toobin, and my FaceTime nether-clamp was way under the Verizon sight line. Risky, but I'm a professional.) Though I had, I realize, been clutching and pacing in the hotel room window. With the lights on. Holding onto my nutsack, in Munich, while the overlord of my life story stood somewhere in Burbank, wielding the knife, nine hours behind me. Why isn't there an International Shame Day?

Before Buchenwald—I should have checked the schedule— we'll be seeing some German wildlife. Specifically, we'll be seeing bears.

That's right. Bears. In a bear pit. Just outside the Hartenfels Castle in Tourgau, in northwest Saxony.

Hartenfels, apparently, is the only Early German Renaissance castle still standing. And I'm not sure how I feel about it. Should any German castles, Early or Late, still be standing? "Hartenfels," the brochure tells us, "was considered to be the most modern residential castle in Saxony in the sixteenth century." Well, wow! Sounds fantastic. Really, I could go on about the grandeur of the palace, the spiral staircase, the, you know, architecture. All the joy to be had clomping up the steps, unchaperoned, to the top of Hausmannsturm tower.

For reasons known only to the gods of Globule, we find ourselves guideless as we roam the exterior. Nor has the threat of ursine sabotage been deemed high enough to merit guards. (Why do I feel, in America, there would be twelve-foot razor-wire fences to keep bear-hating maniacs from leaping over and trying to murder the animals. Or, more likely, leaping over and trying to bond, à la Timothy Treadwell, the bear-loving subject of Werner Herzog's riveting documentary *Grizzly Man*. Spoiler alert: Mr. Treadwell got too close.)

The castle's PR team works overtime to make their bear pit–and-tower attraction the best bear pit–and-tower attraction in the county. "This proud, medieval tower is Hartenfels's highest at fifty-three meters, and connects the late Gothic Albrect building with the Grand John Frederick section . . ."

Germans are such name-droppers! Napoleon, Martin Luther, Tsar Peter I, the irrepressible Johann Friedrich the Magnanimous (AKA John Frederick), and Frederick the Wise all slept at Hartenfels. (Frederick the Dumb, one guesses, couldn't find the place and had to crash in a ditch.)

No doubt true travel sophisticates would head on in to get a look at the famous visitors' accessories. (Oh look, it's Napoleon's truss!) But I'm sorry, I'm shallow. And from the second we hit the joint, my eyes stay locked on one thing and one thing only. The bear pit.

Check it out!

A walkway crosses over the pit, really an infield-sized slab of grass and dirt, about thirty feet beneath, so the rabble can lean over an alarmingly low wall and stare right down at the three brown bears.

Surprisingly (to me), the bears are completely round. The one nearest looks like an enormous feral capon, wrapped in fur. Only two are out and about, and they opt to sit at opposite ends of the yard, doing nothing, plopped down close to the old-timey black barred doors that, if this were a movie, would open directly into the dungeon.

I keep waiting for one of the doors to open and a troll in a loincloth, wielding mace and club, to stagger out and bark up at the tourists, "I fight bear!" Whereupon we shower him with euros and pretzel bits. But no luck.

I hang on the bridge for almost an hour, and can honestly report that the bears just sit there, ignoring each other. For some reason, I think of my Aunt Bess and Uncle Hymie, who (legend has it) lived in the same cabbage-smelling apartment for forty years and never spoke to each other. Unless that was a lie too—like saying there are three bears here at the Hartenfels Castle—and when family wasn't around they sat on each other's laps and cooed.

"Big whoop!" Bob the Bulldozer says, sidling up to join me in bear-gazing. "All they do is sit on their arse and stare at dirt!"

"I've had years like that," I say, without thinking about it, one of those jokes you make reflexively.

"Really?" Bulldozer Bob says, and I can tell he's creeped out. Or maybe concerned.

"Oh, uh, no." I try to smile. "Joke!"

Then, for no reason, I clap him on the back. Which,

considering that we're angled over a low wall, above a pair of bears, is also a weird and, possibly, dangerous thing to do. Even if they seem docile, they're still bears, right? Just ask Herzog.

For one bad second I see panic in Bob's eyes. Nowhere in the Globule literature does it say they screen for psychos, so who knows who I could be? One thing I'm really not is a back-slapper. Least of all when one slap could send the slapee hurtling to a grisly death by bear lunch. I don't know where the urge came from. Lucky, for both of us, Shlomo chooses that moment to sidle up and say hi.

"What do you think?" I ask, grateful to see him.

"What do I think?" Shlomo hikes up his creased too-short mom jeans and gets serious. "Germans love bears. Bear baiting. It's in their history. Wait till we get to Buchenwald. The kommandant there built a bear pit. Threw a Jew in every day."

"What, and the bear would eat them?" Bulldozer Bob goes green around the gills.

"Not all of them. The kommandant kept an eagle in the cage with the bear. And the eagle picked at the bones . . . Jews and bears." Shlomo shakes his head and peers down, sighing, into the scruffy hollow. "Not great."

"Except for the Bear Jew," I tell him, then realize he has no idea what I'm talking about. "From *Inglourious Basterds*?"

Both Shlomo and Bob have blank expressions. I'm ringing no bells with the reference. "It's a Tarantino movie, about Nazi hunters in World War II. One of the Nazi hunters was called the Bear Jew. When they caught a Nazi, if the Nazi didn't do what Brad Pitt wanted, the Bear

Jew swung a baseball bat at his head. You know . . ." I hear myself trail off, "Tarantino?"

"I know about Tarantino," Bob the Bulldozer says.

"I don't." Shlomo sounds put out. "Is that a kind of ice cream?"

There follows silence so awkward I'm almost grateful for Tad, joking in that too-loud way he has, over the bear pit, "I bet if you paid them enough, the landlords at this dump would let you shoot one of these puppies. You could go full Don Junior."

Madge snort-laughs, a thing she does. "Didn't know Junior shoots puppies."

"You know what I mean, Precious. Don Junior shoots wild animals—only they ain't so wild. Somebody tranqs 'em first. Like these bears down there. Looks like they're sleepin' off a three-day fentanyl run."

At first I think the solemn expression on Shlomo's face is a reaction to Tad's stab at humor. Shlomo is, after all, a Trump man. Then I realize it's something deeper.

My older friend gazes forlornly down, like he's staring into the abyss. Which I come to realize he is. "Jews and pits," he mutters softly, "two words you never want in the same sentence."

Now Tad and I are the confused ones.

"What? You think Nazis are the first ones to mass-murder Jews? Think they invented it?"

So begins a history lesson that lasts from that looming moment over Bear Manor to the moment, after a short stroll off the massive castle grounds, when we step from the cobbled street into the open arms of Mother Bus.

"Nearly seven hundred years ago," Shlomo tells us,

"in the Middle Ages, Black Death was wiping out Europe. And guess who people blamed? I'll give you a hint. It wasn't the Eskimos."

Now comes that sly, pants-hitching smile I love so much I could kiss it, followed by a quick tamp-down of the nine strands Shlomo combs carefully back atop his mole and freckle–dappled scalp. And then a shrug as old as Moses. "They needed somebody to blame. So who else? They found some poor old Jew and tortured him into yelping that he'd poisoned the well—what did the goyim know about germs and rats?—and, voilà, pogroms and mass murders in every city and village on the continent. Because they found the cause of the Black Death. And when those Jews were murdered, by beating or shooting or locking them in a barn and setting it on fire, what's left?"

"The bodies." Tad turns around and plants his double chins on the back of his seat. Today, by the way, his T-shirt says, *I See Dumb People!*

"And where do they dump them?" Shlomo asks, employing the Shlo-cratic method.

"In pits," I hear myself say.

There's a long pause, before Shlomo ties it up in a bow. "Jews," he says, "in pits. As far back as the 1300s. And with or without pits, for centuries before, the Church blamed Jews—instead of Romans—for the death of Christ. Don't believe that crap about the Second Vatican Council in 62. Pope Paul may have said Jews weren't guilty, but nobody believed it."

By now Shlomo's staring off, talking, I suspect, more to himself than us. "And I'll tell you what else. The towns that jumped on the Jew-killing bandwagon? They were the first to jump on board later, when the Nazis showed up. I guarantee if there was a Jewish caveman—BAM!—the other cavemen would have conked him with a boulder."

"Y'all are the chosen people," Madge chimes in, offering up her best Pepsodent smile.

"Yeah, right," says Tad, "chosen to get the shit kicked out of you."

Shlomo catches my eye. "It's the little things."

"That's funny," I say, before adding—sometimes you can't worry about sounding stupid—"One thing I've always wondered about the Jews: does God love 'em or hate 'em?"

"Well," says Shlomo, his response nothing short of theatrical—shoulders, eyebrows, and palms all up in a rabbinical shrug—"if you have to ask . . ."

Next stop, Buchenwald.

# CHAPTER 17
## JEDEM DAS SEINE

🚌 🚌 🚌

THE SIGN ON THE BUCHENWALD GATE, *Jedem das Seine,* faces the inside of the camp. This was, allegedly, so the inmates could look up and be reminded of the slave camp's guiding philosophy. Roughly, in English, "To each his own," or "Everyone gets what he deserves." The Nazi equivalent of "You Can't Always Get What You Want," the Stones song that once closed Trump rallies. A mystery for the ages. (Did Mick need the money?)

By now, the parallels between Adolf and Donald are beyond old news. It's not just that both men boasted alarming hair and gamy charisma. In the beginning, except for a handful of racist maniacs and World War I vets, everybody in Germany thought Hitler was an ass clown too.

But back to the present. "To each his own" turns out to be a popular slogan in Germany. A dozen years ago, Esso plastered it on posters advertising coffee at seven hundred gas stations around the country. According to *Der Spiegel,* the Central Council of Jews in Germany declared the ad an example of "total historical ignorance." Not long after, German grocery chain REWE put out a brochure with the catchy tagline, "Barbecuing: To Each His Own." Before, of course, coming forth with a heartfelt apology. "No disrespect to the Jewish people intended."

Our guide, Lena, a lovely millennial who keeps flinging wisps of hair out of her eyes, very Kate Winslet, explains that Buchenwald was not an extermination camp, like its cousin Auschwitz. Inmates weren't gassed, they were worked to death, used as slave labor. Horrific enough, but now that I'm writing this up I can't help but recall how Donald Trump didn't pay his workers, either! But never mind. I promised myself to lay off the Trump stuff.

The macro-horrors of the camps are well known. But the smaller specifics of state torment can be equally haunting. Lena leads us to the pathology lab of the crematorium, in which a doctor's measuring stick has been mounted, vertically, along the wall in the corner. "When the camp was primarily Soviet POWS, Hitler had a directive that the commissars—that's what he called Russians—were all to be shot in the back of the neck. So look closer."

Lena leads us out of the room, to a tiny booth behind the wall where the SS slid their guns through a slot in the measuring stick, and shot the inmates in the backs of their necks. Which, horrifically fascinating as it is, is not even the most salient detail.

Listen: "The kommandant knew that shooting a man point-blank, when he's looking straight at you, could do some psychological damage to the shooter. So they invented the measuring room. Prisoners were told they were being measured for camp uniforms."

The murderous misdirect, of course, was an SS staple. Like telling new arrivals at Auschwitz they were headed for showers.

"By the way," Lena adds, "none of the guards were compelled to join the murder squad. The higher-ups knew that if they were ordered to kill, the men might resist. Might resent the order. But if they volunteered, they were motivated. They wanted to be 'man among men.' There was, you might say, a subtle psychology involved, what today we might call their 'management style.'"

The kommandant of Buchenwald was Karl-Otto Koch, who is more famous for his wife Ilse—AKA the Bitch of Buchenwald. Though Karl himself was no slouch. He made his bones putting men in doghouses; making them kneel and bark; shoving hot tar up their anuses when they broke a rule.

Ilse is famous for a lot of things, among them riding through the camp on her horse in skimpy lingerie, daring any of the starving male inmates she passed to look at her. Those who did, the guards dragged off and shot. This was kind of her thing. She also enlisted teenaged boys as house slaves, and liked to lie in bed naked when they brought her morning Speckpfannkuchen. Again, if one of the teen boys got aroused, or so much as raised his eyes to her, out he went, dragged off to be shot. The boys she would select for actual orgies, she would shoot afterward.

The contrast between the soft cast of the tour guide's voice and the brutal nonfiction it's describing is striking. "But murder and sexual sadism are just the beginning," Lena continues. "Ilse was also obsessed with tattoos. It has been said that when she spotted a tattooed prisoner, she would have him skinned, then keep the skin."

"Good thing she never saw your butt—huh, Madge?" Tad kids. And I can see, on the faces of folks not in our group, mostly Europeans, that familiar expression, the one that says, *Fucking Americans!*

Douglas rolls his eyes and groans, just loud enough, "Oh for God's sake."

"Ooops, sorry," Tad says, and Madge gives him a pretend-angry slap.

"More gruesome still," Lena resumes, "Ilse did not just like to remove the skins, the kommandant's wife liked to use skins for what you Americans, I believe, call 'crafts.' Or is it 'crafting'?"

"Either one," Trudy says, from the corner of our group. "Honey, you're doing great."

"Thank you," Lena says, with a shy smile she gets rid of in half a second. "Buchenwald's liberators found lampshades and book covers made from humans in Ilse's home. They also found boxes of trinkets, made from human leather, which Ilse liked to send out to friends and fellow SS officers at Christmas. The kommandant's wife was oddly partial to shrunken heads, which were found in her living room. And—I hope you all have the strong stomach—in her mansion she used actual human thumbs for light switches."

In evidence at Nuremberg, Lena goes on, were a collection of items created by Frau Koch. Among them those lampshades, "a detail familiar to people who know little else of the Holocaust."

Of course, the lampshades are old news. But thumbs?

"Makes Vlad the Impaler look like Mister Rogers, huh?" Tad says.

Even in an era made callous by decades of *Saw* and *Silence of the Lambs*, something about Ilse's special vices—

her voracious appetite for the absolute worst things you can imagine—packs the ability to shock.

"And she had babies around?" Pam shakes her head, and Trudy picks up the thread. "Hell, they were already living at a concentration camp, I'm guessing the kids were pretty warped."

Trudy shakes her head. "Kids are innocent, even if their parents are sadistic perverts."

"No need to get personal," I say, and instantly regret it.

"You're a bit of a headcase, aren't you," Trudy offers, with what I hope is affection, but I suspect reflects the unfazed, seen-it-all-acceptance of a stone pro with thirty years in the high school trenches, a woman who's plucked her share of cell phones, Nintendo, and porn out of her students' grasp.

Before anyone can smirk, Lena soldiers on, ignoring my nervous blurt. "Since you mention babies"—she aims her words at Pam, pointedly ignoring you-know-who— "Frau Koch raised three children in a large, beautiful house just outside the camp, on a lane called Officers Row. Ultimately, after the war, her son could not reconcile the horror of what his parents did, and killed himself. Two daughters, also attended to by slaves, grew up to marry and move away. Neither ever had anything to do with their mother."

In one of a few satisfying codas to the story, Lena, who speaks with the nerve-tingling, barely-above-a-whisper rasp of an ASMR professional, tells us how, after liberation, General Patton ordered Nazi party officials, and citizens of Weimar, to make their way on foot to the camp. To witness, for themselves, what had gone on there.

"In newsreel footage of the liberation, we can see locals starting off their walk happy, smiling, like they're going to a picnic. We see them stop before the table Patton had set up, studying an array of preserved organs, shrunken skulls, and items made from prisoners' skin. Their expressions change. After this we see the Weimar citizens face-to-face with the bodies of the dead, piled by the hundreds all around the camp. Then we see these locals crying, being sick to their stomachs, and trying to leave. All this, throughout the war, was going on in their neighborhood."

"I see nothing!" Tad exclaims, doing his best Sergeant Schultz, from *Hogan's Heroes*, an American Boomer reference clearly lost on all but a few on hand. But not to me.

"Speaking of Sergeant Schultz," I say to Tad—I can't help myself—"did you know they made a movie version of this whole saga? *Ilsa, She Wolf of the SS*." Heads turn, but nobody looks at all interested except for Tad, my target audience.

"Sounds racy," he says, waggling his eyebrows. Already I'm feeling myself skid down the slope of compulso overshare, but can't stop. "Oh yeah," I babble on, "*Ilsa, She Wolf of the SS*. Made in 1975. Considered the first Nazisploitation film."

I sidle over, passing a frowning Douglas and blinking Shlomo, and get closer to Tad. I'm thinking, in a last-minute grasp at appropriate conversing, maybe it's best to kind of keep this between us. "The crazy thing," I whisper, "it was shot on the set of *Hogan's Heroes*."

"You're messin' with ol' Tad!"

"No! Square business. The show had just been canceled. So the producers agreed to let them shoot there, since the last scene of the movie called for the camp to be burned down, which saved the studio having to shell out to demolish the sets. They shot *Ilsa* in nine days. Then torched the whole joint."

"Gerald, you are a font," Tad says.

I could go on. I could tell him how last night, in a fit of ill-considered creativity, I had the idea to work the story of this grindhouse classic into the treatment for the soon-to-never-go-anywhere pilot about my life. What I've been discussing with the Sensitive Exec. Before I can, however, Madge takes Tad's arm and leads him off. This time she does not even pretend to be amused.

No doubt it's bad tourist behavior, but before we break, I'm moved to ask our well-spoken guide, Lena, why a capable, charismatic young woman like her would choose to work at a concentration camp. Clearly uncomfortable at my liberty, Lena takes a moment and plays with a strand of her hair. Then she answers the question.

"When I was little, my grandfather told me a story about a farmer in town. The farmer was a very kind man. He had also been a Nazi. One day my grandfather asked him, 'You seem so nice, why would you follow Adolf Hitler?' 'Because,' the old farmer told him, 'who else would give me twenty slaves?' I think this is something people don't understand about the Nazis. For regular people, nonpolitical people, there could be enormous benefits."

I wait a beat, expecting her to add, ". . . and that farmer was my grandfather's father." And drop the mic.

But there's no mic drop. What she does is nod, perhaps to herself, before concluding, with simmering conviction, "I believe people should know."

Before I can ask a follow-up, Lena steps away, finds the rest of the group, and asks if they all know where the cafeteria is. Then she suggests we go there for a "delicious luncheon."

I get the distinct impression she does not want to answer any more personal questions.

I cannot, in case you are wondering, bring myself to eat at the Buchenwald cafeteria. (Much classier than the Auschwitz snack bar, with sit-down tables.) I can, however, walk slowly through, after visiting the men's room, and make a point of staring at the diners disapprovingly while flagrantly taking pictures of them. *Look at me,* I am silently declaring, *too noble to eat here, but not too noble to walk by taking pictures and judging you amoral carnivores.* (In hindsight, of course, a total douche move.)

I stomp out of the cafeteria, fast, to show I am so sensitive it bothers me to see people eating where so many suffered.

And then, BAM. Like a fucking idiot, I walk fullspeed into a plate glass sliding door and stagger backward, bleeding from the forehead. Now I have to trot back in, past the diners I have just self-righteously judged, back to the Buchenwald men's room—also nicer than the crude facilities at Auschwitz (that's Germany versus Poland right there)—where I grab a fistful of wet paper towels and try to staunch the blood streaming over my unibrow.

The realization that, even here, at the Axis Mundi of My People's Agony, I have managed to make an ass out of myself, is not a great feeling.

Stunned and ashamed, I wobble off and spot an unexpected cigarette machine in a corner of the café, so old it looks like it might have had a cameo in *Ocean's Eleven*, the Sinatra and Lawford version. Instead of buying smokes—it's been thirty years since my last Lucky—I just lay my head on top of the machine, realize I've left a blood puddle, then sop it up and paddle back out, keeping my eyes straight ahead, careful about the door this time.

I drift outside, blinking in the sunlight, and run smack into Patsy, who eyes my head wound with jocular disbelief. "Ouch," she laughs, "have a bit of a dustup, Gerald?"

"Long story."

Turns out she's a well-prepared traveler, and digs some Polysporin and Band-Aids out of her kit bag. After I'm patched up, Patsy hands me an extra bandage—just in case—and heads off, calling over her shoulder, "Try not to lose an eyeball, mate."

Thus chastened, I make my way toward one of the two guard towers left intact by the east entrance gate. (Originally, there were twenty-two.) Oddly, the towers are rustic, three-level constructions: stucco on the bottom, then a layer of dark wood, and above that, windows. But not the kind you'd expect. These aren't the gun-turret towers familiar to those, say, who've had occasion to visit some of America's finer penitentiaries, or fans of prison movies. They're less menacing than bucolic. This, in a way, makes them *more* menacing, like the camp itself: set on the northern slope of a mild hill called Ettersberg, in the woods where Goethe used to like to wander around, collecting leaves and cooking up *Faust*, the play that would birth the phrase "Faustian bargain."

One wonders (and is it possible to write "one wonders" without one wanting to leap out of one's chair, change one's name to Aleister, and begin dressing one entirely in scratchy tweed?) if Young Johann, the pride of Weimar, birthplace of the nineteenth-century German liberal tradition, ever sat under a tree after tromping around the Thuringian Forest, picked a flower, then looked up and saw a nation of Fausts, fifty years down the road, who would act out the terms of their bargain in blood—some of them right here in lovely Ettersberg.

At Nuremberg, the number of concentration camp guards who were actually tried, let alone stuck with sizable jail time, was in low double figures. I want to say twelve.

Like a big old SS gazebo for trained killers, each tower has these old-fashioned, small glass windows in two rectangular sections below a black roof that comes to a point in the middle.

Hard as I stare, I still can't figure out if the windows open inward or outward, or how they aimed the rifles. But I lack the moxie to climb up and find out. (At least not sober.) Guards had orders to shoot any inmate who got within a hundred feet of the electrified barbed-wire fence. Apparently hundreds tried to escape. Though it's not clear to me why guards would have shot them, since they could have just let the inmates run and fry themselves on the fence. Either way, you were going to die. But perhaps even those last moments of free will were more than camp management were willing to cede.

That I, with my soft-ass life of nothing more than financial, nuptial, psycho-emotional, and physical white-guy woes, would find myself five minutes later wondering if the fence still had frying power, so I could just drop my dumb-fuck shoulder bag—full of soon-to-be-lost scribbled-in notebooks—and run for the juice, is not something I'm proud of. But I can tell you why I wished it. Because, standing here, breathing in the excruciating, insensate quiet of these pastoral former killing fields, I hear the beep of my iPhone and reflexively grab it. Instead of doing the right thing, ignoring it. Out of respect for where I am. For what's happened here. But no. I check the message, and read the text from my tender network executive: *Can you make Jerry less creepy?*

Oof!

And a second later, before this completely sinks in, another few words: *That voice-over!!! Dude, you're scaring people.*

Jesus.

# CHAPTER 18
## *HOW CAN THE DEAD RESPECT THE LIVING?*

🚌 🚌 🚌

ALL AROUND US, THE BLOOD of the past screams to the present.

Do the dead, I wonder, ever look up at the living and think, *What the fuck are you doing?* There is infinite respect for the dead, but do they—can they—reciprocate and respect the living? Not all of them, if I had to guess.

Meaning and portent everywhere. But I can't help myself, and instantly hunch over my phone and fumble to find the attachment in my Sent box, the latest and clearly next-level-repellant version of the ABC series treatment. (This was before I realized that nothing I could write, nothing that came from me, nothing about me, would ever please these people. But why rush the inevitable?)

"Here we go," I say out loud. Then reading, careful not to move my lips: "Open on Jerry up to his neck in Nazi research at his desk, papers everywhere, facing a computer. A three-year-old girl plays on the floor near him." I skip the rest of the exposition and scroll down to the offending voice-over:

*Jerry VO: "I was scoping Nazi enema bondage, little Zelda playing at my feet, when it hit me, I'm* going to hell! *This was research. It could pay for college. But still . . . This had to be some kind of moral travesty. On the other hand, we were eating gummy bears, and she was coloring Winnie-the-Pooh. I don't think she ever looked up. If she did, I suppose, the psycho-emotional fallout probably wouldn't kick in for twenty years. That's the thing about being an Old Guy dad. You probably won't be around to see how things turn out with your Old Guy baby. Thank God. And thank God for said baby's forgiving, maternally superpowered mom.*"

Well, okay. It's not Harold Pinter . . .

As if he's heard me ruminate, and wants to answer, the phone rings. It's Sensitive Exec. He's switched from text to actual human-to-human interaction. Bold!

I pick up, and he launches in: "That voice-over! Can you explain what you were going for here?"

"Sure," I blunder forward, ignoring his tone, "so Jerry has this idea for a movie about the making of the cult classic *Ilsa, She Wolf of the SS.* The movie was shot in Culver City, on the abandoned *Hogan's Heroes* lot. I was just telling somebody about it. As a matter of fact, I'm standing where the actual Ilse wreaked her savage havoc."

"Savage what? Where did you say you were?"

"In Germany. In the real prison camp, Buchenwald, where the real Bitch of Buchenwald lived and murdered."

"I'm sorry . . . Where are you? Bloomingdales? *I said stevia, Marcie!*"

"I'm at . . . never mind. Not important. The point is, in the process of researching, Jerry discovers this whole subgenre of soft-core Nazisploitation. It's a real rabbit hole, so he's got all these crazy books and clips."

"Um," he says, after a beat, "are you serious right now?"

"What do you mean?"

He sputters, as if just having the words in his mouth is giving him toxic shock syndrome. "SS enema bondage? This is ABC. I mean, come on!"

By now I am squeezing and shaking the phone. *Fuck!*

I spot another tour group, stopped on the main track fifty feet way. I believe they're Korean folk. I do not realize I'm just standing there squeezing and shaking, until I see that they are all staring at me. Before quickly, when they see me staring back, turning their heads and walking away in single file.

It's all I can do to keep from running over, crashing their group, and pleading with them. I want to tell the Koreans the story, tell *them* how the pilot opens with me looking at weird-ass Nazi stuff, with my toddler on the floor coloring.

All true—but who cares? Sensitive hates it. I'm not sure about the Koreans—though who can say? Maybe they're sophisticates. (I once heard a Flying Wallenda say he found gravity insulting. Which either makes sense or doesn't.)

"Hang on," says Sensitive. And for some reason, while standing on the killing ground, staring off, I think about Jerry Lewis.

As one does.

The one thing I know—and like—about Jerry Lewis is that after a meeting, he would pretend to forget his attaché case, which was actually a tape recorder. Then he'd come back in fifteen minutes, retrieve the case, and sit in his car listening to what whoever he had the meeting with said about him after he left the room.

Personally, I wouldn't want to hear. What people think about me. I don't even want to hear what *I* think of me. Is the secret-agent case even necessary? Don't you kind of just *know?*

(Speaking of Jerry, how can we not mention *The Day the Clown Cried*, his uber-kitsch Holocaust epic, in which he plays a death camp clown, cheering up children on the way to the showers? So far, like my pilot, it has never seen the light of day either.)

But where was I?

I forget that I've been holding, until Sensitive speaks up again.

"We can't do this," Sensitive declares. "We can't do any of it."

"But," I hear myself begin, and then stop. But *what?*

I hold the phone, stare off, yet again, at the bare counting grounds. Where inmates lined up every morning in the freezing cold, for those endless hours.

What are the odds, all these years later, some foreigner would be standing where they stood and pitching a story about the kommandant's wife? As B story in a sitcom?

By now I'm sweating. One wrong move, seventy years ago, and a man standing where I'm standing—if he had tattoos—could end up as a wallet. Instead, it's seventy years later, I've got the ink, and I'm on a cell phone, waiting for a different verdict. I feel woozy. There is no deodorant for desperation.

Now comes the moment of truth: does the artist (is this *art?*) take a stand, go noble, boldly insist, "Either this story's told the way I want to tell it, or I'm not telling it all"? All *Mr. Smith Goes to Hollywood*? Or does he, seized by fear, alimony, child support, college funds, mortgage . . . all the bourgeois ball-squeezers, try to keep going; try, you know, to *please* the corporate beast. Come up with something, *anything* . . . Because, you know, it could work, it might. I mean it's doubtful, it's actually unlikely, but still. Maybe. (*Daddy, why can't I have oboe lessons anymore?*) Maybe now's not the time to think about the novel you should be writing. (To paraphrase the playwright Richard Greenberg, "Money doesn't buy you happiness. But it does upgrade despair.") Or not. Maybe now's the time for some Buddhist nonattachment. Though what, exactly, is being nonattached? Integrity? Delusion? Heat rash? Can epigenetic agita leak through your DNA and trickle out like flop sweat? At twenty-two, I remember thinking, *Did my poor dead father dodge pogroms, journey through Ellis Island, struggle up the ladder so his son could graduate college and write fake sex letters for* Penthouse Forum?

"Dear Penthouse, *My girlfriend has a bush like Castro's beard, and we were on a Ferris wheel . . .*"

"Dear Penthouse, *When I have sex I think about death . . .*"

Do the departed know things that would make the living feel ashamed?

What would the dead tell us if they could speak?

"*Good talk.*"

What?

Has Sensitive been talking this whole time?

"Uh . . . Jerry?"

"Right here!" *Shit.*

"Okay, good stuff. Glad you called, got another call."

"Did I call you?"

"What?"

"Um . . . nothing, nothing."

Fuck! Do other people wonder if they're screaming out loud? I feel, absurdly, like I've just sprouted a shame-based blastoma. Right on top of my brain.

"Good talk," Sensitive repeats, and I realize I have no idea what he's been saying. Haven't heard a word. "We'll pick this up."

"Good stuff," I say, and hang up.

A thought careens in my brain: *It all feels wrong*.

How many victims, buried under my feet right now, worried that they were frauds? Living the wrong life? Self-sabotagers and wimps, manipulators and goons and outright swine, along, of course, with heroes, solid family men, and all the prematurely dead in between.

Jew-to-Jew, I'm losing it. But I want to know. I need to. Did these victims, before they were victims, just want to get things *right*? How long, after they were thrown in the camp, was the privilege of idiot self-obsession stripped away?

How long before they realized the futility of all those wasted hours thinking about sex and money, did their hair look right, success and failure and all the things that drain the life out of life—when life itself is so fucking vulnerable and fragile and easy to pluck away? How long did regret and longing linger in the face of elemental terrors: hunger, cold, imminent, undeserving death?

Bad enough I'd been thinking about that Nazi sitcom in the middle of Buchenwald. Worse, I'm thinking about myself. The ball of regret I carry with me will not fit in my

Bluesmart suitcase, so I carry it in my stomach. (Can this be helped, the author asks defensively, when we all keep little me-machines in our pocket? Your smartphone isn't smart enough to know when you're not supposed to look at it. It doesn't know about the camps, or what's appropriate and what's evidence of borderline personality. Where is the app that measures your crumbling soul?)

Insanely, again, I want to make a run for the fence. I know I won't be electrocuted, but the relief of thinking I might be, as I'm hauling ass to the barbed wire, makes the dash hard to resist. In the long litany of things a visit to a death camp will reveal about the visitor, that there's no off switch on self-obsession is one of the more painful. (I hope you can't relate.)

I do not even realize that I'm walking in tight little circles until I hear that familiar "Oy!"

I turn, and it's Shlomo. He seems alarmed. "Boychick, you look like you just saw a ghost! And your head is bleeding!"

I touch my forehead, where I'd banged it in the camp dining room. "Oh shit!"

No wonder the Koreans looked at me like I'd escaped a Stephen King movie.

"Maybe *I'm* the ghost," I say, as he pulls out a plaid hanky and dabs my forehead. (Who carries a hanky?)

"You're no ghost, boychick. I've seen you eat."

"You're right. Forget it."

Sick of thinking about myself, I notice my old pal scratching vigorously at the back of his hand and ask what's up.

"Concentration camp mosquitoes," he tells me, after

a beat. "The worst kind." He thinks another minute, as if deciding if he wants to speak what's on his mind, then just says it: "You know, you were talking to yourself."

"I was?"

"Forget it. This is a terrible place." Then Shlomo leans close and whispers, a gleam in his eye I haven't seen before, "How about that Ilse, huh?"

"Ilse?"

"What a firecracker!"

# CHAPTER 19
## *WALKING INTO GLASS*

🚌 🚌 🚌

LATER THAT AFTERNOON, when we gather outside the Buchenwald restaurant, I have to explain my bloody forehead to my concerned (and weirded-out) companions. I try a stigmata joke, which goes nowhere, and finally tell them the truth: "I walked into a plate glass door."

"And he's the one who don't drink!" cracks Tad.

"Good one!" says Patsy, who had in fact helped me tamp the blood when I'd first banged myself. She'd already puked in front of me, so I guess, in an Australian kind of way, we'd bonded. There's some good-natured ribbing, as Bulldozer Bob piles on: "Yeah, nah, if this is him sober, give him a drink, he'd probably be in a bleedin' heap, wouldn't he?"

"Oh snap," Trudy says.

I try to laugh right along. But, in case the whole situation isn't awkward enough, my busmates, mistaking the stricken look on my post–Sensitive Exec call face as some kind of flesh-wound angst, try to cheer me up. Or worse, show concern.

"Gerald, are you okay?" Don seems to scowl as he inquires, with that I-know-all-about-you attitude common to all cops, state or otherwise.

I'm grateful when Douglas steps in on my behalf. "Gerald's fine." Then he calls me the Hero of Munich for helping him track down Tito yesterday.

"But I wasn't lost!" Tito responds, his bewildered tone successfully shifting the focus away from me and my injury.

For the first time in my life, I understand the term "happy campers." And I'm in a concentration camp.

Leading off our postlunch exploration is the crematorium. Recalling, with no small self-disgust, my reaction to the last crematorium, the whole Bobby and Marla pizza incident, I'm glad I'm seeing this one with my group.

Lena reels off some more facts and details as we stroll across the grounds, a gentle breeze blowing from the leafy woods just past the perimeter, and that electric gate. The sky's so blue it feels inappropriate.

"Over there," she says, pointing to the right, "is Goethe's stump."

"Where's the rest of him?" Tad jokes. Not his best material.

We all turn dutifully to see the hollowed bottom of what must have once been an enormous tree, and hear the story behind it. "This is also known as Goethe's Oak. When the camp was built, the SS let the giant tree remain, in honor of Goethe himself, who is said to have loved to sit beneath it, composing poetry. It was destroyed when the Allies bombed the camp in 1944, targeting the factory where slave labor manufactured V-2 rocket parts. But as you can see, the stump remains."

I'm not sure the point of the story. Unless it's that the

SS had a poetic side, and loved to curl up with *The Sorrows of Young Werther* when not beating inmates to death or making them stand naked in the snow until their toes fell off, or hypothermia killed them.

"An interesting thing about Buchenwald," Lena goes on as we stroll along, "when construction began in the summer of 1937, prisoners themselves were tasked with building it."

Her voice, somehow, has dropped to a more low-key, hypnotic timbre since lunch. That, or banging my head has affected my hearing.

A moment later we arrive at the crematorium. Lena stops before entering. "Can anybody," she asks, "quite imagine what it feels like to build the crematorium where you yourself might someday burn?"

We stand in silence, staring down at our comfortable shoes, until she continues. "It's important to remember that, along with housing enemies of the state, Buchenwald was a cutting-edge military complex for training SS Totenkopf units. Totenkopf means 'death's head.' And these were the most violent, and also the most revered, branch of the SS. To join, a soldier had to stand at least six feet tall and have papers proving one hundred years of pure Aryan stock. For such pure Aryans, the inmates—communists, Jews, Gypsies, homosexuals, Jehovah's Witnesses—were considered not to be human, but to be filth, vermin, garbage. So, to these men, the room we are about to enter was a place for burning garbage."

"Bleak," someone mutters. I don't know who.

The tour has taken an abrupt turn from Goethe's happy tree. But to me it's perfect. My sense is, disgusted by the too-flip demeanor of so many Americans to the scene at hand, but too classy to remark on it, our guide wants to lower the hammer.

"The ovens had the operating ability to dispose of four hundred bodies every ten hours. Before they were burned, all body cavities were searched for treasure. The SS found it easier to remove gold teeth before the corpses were pushed into the fire."

No remarks now. Nothing but the slow drill of simple fact piercing deeper and deeper into the visitor's soul.

Cadaver stats dispensed with, now comes the mundane detail that renders the whole in perfect perspective. Lena steps close to one of the ovens, and points. There it is. The company that made the ovens, *J.A. TOPF & SÖHNE* (Sons), saw fit to inscribe its name proudly on their equipment, on a little plaque. Topf, it turns out, was the biggest maker of bakery ovens in Germany. And really, why wouldn't the purveyors of machinery that kept the fatherland in cheesecake and streuselkuchen want its mass-murder-adjacent accomplishments known?

*Yes, we made the ovens,* Topf & Sons want you to know, *and we're damn proud of it.* Every dead man shoved in the hell-cave had to slide right by that little brass plaque, reminder of their corporate heat. Perhaps part of the deal is that the plaques stay polished.

Amazingly, Topf actually went out of business. Unlike Mercedes, Volkswagen, Bayer, IG Faber, Hugo Boss, and other enablers of the Nazi project, who are all doing fine. What's a little slave labor among friends? Think about that the next time you have a headache, or need a nice bar mitzvah suit.

Lena concludes the lesson with one of the beyond-the-camp details that make her such an entertaining (if entertaining is the word) Virgil to our pack of bus-riding Dantes. "After the war, a trove of correspondence from the oven company to the SS turned up. At the end of every letter, the Topf team would sign off the same way, *Stets gern für Sie beschäftigt . . . Always happy to be at your service.*" The tone, for lack of a better term, is chipper.

After the war, the company was taken away from the Topfs. By 2001 the corporate headquarters building was still empty, when a group of radical young squatters decided to move in—the Topf Collective—transforming the place into a kind of cultural center for "far-out performances," as well as a place to live. Eventually, like many genocide-related sites, it became a memorial center, which it remains.

"I like that ending," Douglas says. More than once, he has complained that Suzannah talks too fast and crams in too many facts. By contrast, Lena's cadence is slow and patient, as if she herself is still coming to terms with the subject at hand.

"Actually," Lena now says, "this is not the end of the story. Dagmar Topf, whose ancestors were the original father-and-son owners, went to court in 1990, when the wall came down, to file a claim that her family deserves to get the property back. It was seized from her, she argues, just as the Jews had their property seized when the Nazis came to power." She waits a beat, her timing perfect, before continuing: "But we do not think her case has a—how do you say?—prayer in hell."

"That's called chutzpah," Tad announces, busting out his trove of Texas Yiddish. "I love it!"

"He loves it," Lena laughs, or makes a sound like a laugh. "Good one."

Is it me, or are nerves fraying all around. Is there snark?

"Okay, let's talk about Germany," Lena resumes. "Not just the Totenkopf but all of Germany felt itself to be the best in the world. This is the irony. In the twenties and thirties, Germany was considered to have the best medical training facilities in the world."

Here, Pam, to everyone's surprise, pops her hand up, lapsing into classroom behavior. "My great-great-grandfather was a doctor, and my grandmother said he was very proud that he had studied medicine over here. It's what all the top doctors did. He came over here and studied stomachs."

"Stomachs?" Douglas sounds almost indignant.

"What's wrong with stomachs?" Tito asks. "The Krauts invented Alka-Seltzer."

"Oh for God's sake," Pam sighs. It's pretty clear, at this point, the woman wishes she'd just kept her mouth shut. But she plows on anyway: "Today we'd call it internal medicine. But my mother always told me that Great-Great-Grandpa Swerton was the best stomach man in Omaha. And he kept his German diploma on the wall above his desk."

"Well I hope it wasn't from U. Buchenwald."

"Trudy!"

"Well was it?" Trudy persists.

I can't tell if the look she's giving her best friend is concerned or joshing. Her eyes are crinkled, like she's going to smile, but the set of her lips is tight and hard. If I were a sixth grader and she aimed that mouth at me, I would probably empty my pockets and flee.

"Heidelberg, 1927," Pam says flatly, then glances at the ceiling, as if doing the math on an overhead blackboard. "I lied. I guess he was my great-great-*great*-grandfather. All those greats get confusing. I do remember, he said he was the only kid from the University of Nebraska—go Huskers! From any state school. He said all the other American med students were from Harvard, Princeton, and Yale."

"That makes the point," Lena says, grabbing the reins back with seasoned élan. "Besides Ilse Koch, who was simply a sadist, at Buchenwald those 'best doctors in the world'"—picture the air quotes—"were doing"—more air quotes—"'research' in the special barracks in the northern part of the camp."

I'd noticed, the more intense the details, the more blank our young chaperone's face. What she was about to say drained all expression from her features. "So-called research included castrating homosexuals, followed by hormone injections to quote-unquote 'cure them of their sexual tendencies.'"

At that moment, I wonder if anybody else feels what I feel: surprise that some John Hagee/Paula White–style right-wing evangelist, some family-values titan whose views on the "homosexual lifestyle" echo the Reich's, has not glommed onto the Nazis' doctors' methods and tried to implement them in America. (I can't help myself: in my head I hear Trump's inflection, announcing his executive castration order on Fox. *"It's incredible! They actually thank you for it, they really do!"*)

When Lena moves on to "experiments with poison

bullets," I catch myself zoning out, then zoning back in time to hear "black boils" and "immediate autopsies."

I watch the grisly info wash over my fellow tourists. Perhaps there is only so much horror that can be absorbed.

In a world of *Saw 1* through *8*, where torture and pain come recreated and marketed as entertainment, how can it be that our senses are *not* numbed? Of course, the fact that the camps were, you know, *real*, that the unspeakable torments actually happened, is supposed to put them in a different league. But while we know this rationally, might our neural pathways be so jaded and crap-encrusted as to be dulled to the effects of genuine horror? So-called "real life"?

I'm reminded of a joke I have heard alternately attributed to Slavoj Žižek, Gilbert Gottfried, or Ricky Gervais. Roughly recounted, in mutilated form: An elderly survivor of the camps dies and goes to heaven. At the pearly gates, he meets God and tells Him a Holocaust joke. God says, "That's not funny." And the survivor says, "I guess you had to be there . . ."

Is this, in some wretched trickle-down way, a philosophical comment on dark tourism as testament to the failure of neoliberalism? The intersection of faithlessness, Borscht Belt existentialism, and dread? Or have I lost my mind entirely? Because it is true: once you spend too much time mulling, obsessing, marinating in any subject, but especially genocide, you can lose it completely. Which may, or may not, serve as my defense for whatever monstrous gibberish may have leaked into the pages you hold in your hand.

I have already begun to see the fatigue that sets in

when the sheer quantity of hellacious info simply over-
flows what your basic human psyche can contain. Still, the
brain finds workarounds.

When tour-guide Lena moves on to phosphorus
burns, inflicted deliberately to test the efficiency of Nazi
balms on the effects of incendiary weapons, I can't help
but think of Phan Thị Kim Phúc, AKA the Napalm Girl,
whose image personalized America's own incendiary
madness in the sixties and seventies in Vietnam. It's the
same sensation you get knowing about Nazis' forced ster-
ilizations, then learning about involuntary hysterectomies
performed on migrant women at the ICE detention center in Ocila, Georgia. In 20-fucking-20. The conclusion
being, when it comes to inflicting horror, the difference
is one of degree. (Georgia's uterus collector, after all, was
simply continuing the policy stated by legal legend Oliver "Three Generations of Imbeciles Is Enough" Wen-
dell Holmes back in *Buck v. Bell*, in 1927.) You could say
there's nothing like the scale of the Nazis, and then you
could say "yet." Either way, crack open *Mein Kampf,* and
there's no denying that America's affection for involuntary
sterilization—and eugenics—was an inspiration for the
short-lived master race. Old news. Dead Jews.

The final tally, we learn: from July 1937, when Buchenwald opened, to April 1945, when it closed, the camp
imprisoned 250,000. The SS murdered, conservatively,
56,000, of which 11,000 were Jewish.

But—and for this I applaud her—Lena concludes
this portion of the proceedings on a positive, or at least
within-shouting-distance-of-positive note. Among the
20,000 survivors at liberation, some one thousand, she

announces, were boys under fourteen. "This tells us that, despite their own horrifying ordeals, the adult men did what they could to keep the young ones alive. That meant giving them portions of food, or clothing, whatever small help they could give." It's an ennobling story. And strikes a different final note than Primo Levi's observation (made long before he threw himself down three flights of stairs in his Turin apartment building): "The worst survived, the selfish, the violent, the insensitive . . . the spies. It was not a certain rule . . . but it was, nevertheless, a rule . . . The best all died."

What moves me is how much our guide wanted to find something, anything, to lift the inexorable weight of the old news she's chosen to make her living dispensing. I don't know if you'd call this compassion, or something else. Whatever it is, I admire her for it.

# CHAPTER 20
## IN NAZI TIMES . . .

🚌 🚌 🚌

POST-BUCHENWALD, WE'LL BE STOPPING at another station of the Nazi cross: Nuremberg.

Suzannah preps us for the experience from her perch up front. By now, I've grown to really enjoy her Driver's Side chats, and find myself looking forward to them with childlike anticipation. Most of our family trips, when I was a child, involved my mother smoking while she drove, and my father, God bless him, hunkered in the passenger seat seething. Not just because his wife wouldn't let him drive—no small public humiliation in the fifties and sixties—but because, once she lit up, my mother liked to keep the windows sealed, so no one could breathe.

We drove in long periods of silence, punctuated by Mom demanding another cigarette, which she'd do, for no apparent reason, in her own brand of truly peculiar faux-beatnik jargon. Her favorite—"Fling me a fag, Dad!"—never failed to get a rise from my sister and me, before we'd start our exaggerated gagging as the smoke filled our ventilation-free Plymouth Valiant and we both got groggy. (Later, when I read about the Nazis' mobile monoxide vans, created to kill Jews by piping the exhaust from the tailpipe directly into the sealed-off vans, my first thought, before the awfulness—and efficiency—of the entire concept, was of those endless, headachy trips, captive of Kommandant Mom, breathing in the tar and nicotine until we did, in fact, feel on the brink of expiring.)

My father, relegated to holder of the Kents, would hand over a cigarette, then resume staring forward at some grim middle distance until his wife stubbed out the smoke, and windows could be rolled down again.

Suzannah's perky narration, I suppose, compensates for that early childhood full of choking, automotive silence. Hence my all but complete regression—I'm surprised I didn't suck my thumb, though I may well have—as our Guidess in Chief launched into whatever tale she was telling on that particular leg of the journey.

Even now, I can hear her opening words. "In Nazi times," Suzannah begins, the same way a mother (just not mine) might begin a story to a sleepy child. It's as weirdly soothing as if she'd gently cooed, *"Once upon a time . . ."* And I'm not alone. I see Shlomo curl up sideways, though it's ten in the morning, his head against a pillow. Like W, Shlo packed a travel pillow, so that wherever he goes, come nighttime, he can breathe in the familiar waft of his own scent, resting his keppie on a little piece of home.

"In Nazi times, Nuremberg was famous as the place where the Nuremberg race laws were drawn up. These were the laws that denied Jews citizenship, Aryanized all rights and property, and forbade Jews from marrying or having sexual relations with persons of German blood." (On the plus side, this would have put the kibosh on my second marriage.)

She goes on to explain that the city was made more

famous when Leni Riefenstahl chronicled its 1935 Nazi Party Congress, attended by more than 700,000 Nazi supporters, in her documentary, *Triumph of the Will.* "The movie captured the unprecedented power and spectacle of the Third Reich rallies in Zeppelin Field. These featured a cathedral of light made by 130 high-power antiaircraft searchlights, visible as far away as Prague, along with endless columns of marching soldiers, fantastically large-scale choreography forming human swastikas, plus hundred-foot-high swastikas and eagles, conjuring images of Roman centurions, and the energy of that endless sea of faces shouting and staring adoringly up at Adolf Hitler."

Suzannah can get poetic. Rhapsodic even, as she lets us know that *Triumph* is considered not just the greatest propaganda ever made, but one of the greatest films period. How it made Riefenstahl the premier female director of her day. Ever impressive with her stats and factoids, Suzannah finishes up, sans notes: "*Triumph of the Will* cost over a million dollars, required nine aerial photographers, thirty cameras, and thirty-six cameramen, some disguised as SS so they could blend in."

"Sounds like a Superbowl halftime show—except for the SS stuff," Madge quips, to much jocularity.

Inspired by her chiming in, I march out my own Riefenstahl story. About how, a week before I left for Poland, I ran into Bud Cort, getting takeout soup at a joint called (what else) Modern Eats, not far from my house. (Hey, I don't love namedropping, either. But I'm going to own this one. Bud is mostly famous for *Harold and Maude*, though he's done a ton of other cool work only his fans know about.)

I knew the actor to nod to, maybe share the odd pleasantry in the Trader Joe's checkout line. But when I mentioned, oversharing as one does when freshly caffeinated, that I was headed off on a Holocaust bus tour, Bud said he had a story he had to tell me. Whereupon he busted out a ridiculous anecdote about going to Germany with Elvis's—or was it Brando's?—photographer (!) and meeting Leni Riefenstahl. They had pastries, he said. Or I *think* he said; they may have had bundt cake. (That part could be whole-cloth wrong.) The point is, she was polite but a little stiff. Until, just as Bud was walking out, the ninetysomething *Triumph of the Will* director perked up and put her elegant crone's claw on his arm, pulling him close. "One thing nobody knows about Hitler," she said, and gave him a squeeze, "he had a great sense of humor!"

Recounting Bud's story, on the bus, I even do the accent—pronouncing "one" "*vun*"—and clench my sphincter as I wait for the laugh after landing the punch line. Before dying like a ninth-rate comic at open-mic night at Chuckles in Allentown.

Suzannah continues as if I haven't said a word, while I sit back and will myself into motor-coach upholstery.

Because Nuremberg hosted these massive displays of Nazi power, the Allies thought it would be the perfect spot to stage their trials, and rub the top Nazis' noses in it. "Of course, mostly why people know Nuremberg is because Nazis were hanged there."

I am still so mortified over my failed anecdote, I could jump up and hug Tad when he launches into his own clunker: "Hell, in my old hometown, Marietta, Georgia, they lynched that Jewboy—beg your pardon, Jewish fella—in 1915. Leo Frank. He was hanged by a mob, but it wasn't good ol' boys, it was what they used to call 'prominent citizens.' Like the mayor. Guys in ties. It's not like old Adolf invented Jew-hatin'. Around Georgia, back in the day, folks called Marietta a hangin' kind of town."

It's a completely egregious anecdote. And highlights, among other travesties, the fact that there is only one person of color on the tour, Mariko, the Japanese American whom Shlomo consulted about Chinese cuisine.

I'm still trying to think all this through when I see Madge pull her Texas Rangers cap down low, then tilt her head back just enough so she can eyeball her hubby from under the brim. "Tad, honey, I wouldn't be braggin' about your hometown hangings," she says, then pulls the brim down lower.

To which Tad responds, "Awww, am I embarrassing you, Peach Cake?"

"You're embarrassing *you*," Madge says, and now everybody in range is staring out the window or at their shoes. It's so awkward, even Suzannah stops talking. Until a voice pipes up, three rows away, "Stop, please! I signed on to this thing to get away from all that."

Heads turn to see Marvin, last seen planting his foot on a Kraków rabbi's tombstone while tying his Nike. "I'm a new divorcé, okay? This is stressful!"

Before I can offer my encouragement—*Don't worry, it gets better, I've been divorced a ton!*—Tad himself snaps at the tombstone stomper: "Thanks for sharing, Marvin, I'll keep that in mind."

Marvin, whose face for some reason always looks like it's been freshly scrubbed, blushes deep scarlet, and clamps his lips tightly shut. This is the first real moment of tension, except for my own private angst over reenacting "'The cheese stands alone" when summoned to sit by myself up front the very first day.

No surprise, besides the odd blurt or whinny, I've become the weird guy who doesn't talk much on the bus. I try to front that I'm gripped by torment, soul-savaged by the overwhelming in-your-faceness of strolling the landscape where Hitler ripped the world apart like a child tearing the head off a doll. Which is partly genuine, partly—mostly—your author's grim, sociopathic tendency to shut down like an unplugged Roomba when planted in the Axis of Planned Activity.

More tense seconds, until Suzannah, who's no doubt learned how to defuse domestic strife in tour-guide school, declaims, in her plummiest of tones, "All right, children, let's get back to business, shall we?"

The ride settles, more or less, back to normal. I see Marvin's face fade to its usual starchy white. And by the time we get to Nuremberg, emerging out of the Franconia uplands, on the Pegnitz river—as lovely as it sounds—no one seems to be hating on anyone else. At least not overtly.

The sky is now a punishing azure, and not for the first time I have the dumb thought: *This is the same sun that stared down at the Nazis.* A notion about as profound as mulch. Which may or may not portend that some age-based, or Nazi-triggered, cognitive decline is in the mail. Maybe, after thinking too much about Hitler, you *want* some cognitive decline. Or maybe the problem, right now, isn't Hitler—it's the human condition, professional stress, rheumatism (Quasimodo elbows), doom (we're in the

Biden Pre-disappointment Months), simply knowing my little girl is going to grow up a thousand miles away. I'm just not thinking right.

(When I wrote this, I should tell you, I had not seen my now-nine-year-old little daughter in over a year. Due to COVID—not to date the whole endeavor—travel was off the table. Getting on a plane felt as appealing as licking the seat in an Uber. When we FaceTimed, she would show me her new tricks. She'd decided she wanted to be a ventriloquist; and, to my surprise, seemed to have mastered half the art of making her words come out of a puppet basenji's mouth. Which is disconcerting, if sweet. "My name is Woof-puss, I miss you, Daddy, can you give me a snack?"

"I only have dinosaur bones."

"Tyrannosaurus Snax," she says, and cracks herself up. That laugh . . . Forgive me if I get Hallmark.)

# CHAPTER 21
## JUDGMENTAL AT NUREMBERG

🚌 🚌 🚌

THERE IS A STRANGE ANTICIPATION as we pull into the Nuremberg Palace of Justice. It's yet another gigantic Bavarian structure, distant cousin to the Hartenfels Castle, minus the bear pit (unless it's hidden), and, Suzannah tells us, the one civic building left standing after allied bombing.

We turistas are left to fend for ourselves in the great Gothic hall, as we were at Hartenfels, dodging plump little bears. One of the highlights is the chance to sit in Room 600, the actual courtroom where Göring and company sat. Hitler's jumbo Luftwaffe ace, incidentally, is shown in the adjoining museum, in news photos, sporting a pair of sunglasses that would not look out of place at Cannes, accessorizing the starring role in which he clearly saw himself, even at the end. (An end Fat Hermann, as he was known, selected himself, crunching a smuggled-in cyanide ampule the night before he was scheduled to hang.)

Having seen the polished and imposing courtroom so many times—most notably, pretour, in an Alec Baldwin miniseries about the trial, where he falls in love with his secretary (the *Guardian* called it *Sleepless in Nuremberg*)—there's the familiar, hard-to-pin-down sensation of knowing that actual world-changing moments of history *happened right here.* That history plunked its corrupt and murderous ass on these very chairs. As if the furniture itself radiates the energy of bygone evil, like the ground at Auschwitz, the ovens in Buchenwald, and pretty much every square inch of fucking Germany and Poland.

The truth, outside of the witness box and judges' dais and disturbing (to me) cross on the wall, I don't remember much of what I saw. For the simple reason that before I got there, I had seen it already. Rendering, perversely, one of the most profoundly charged locations in history at once physically ho-hum, and psychically searing. Climactic and anticlimactic at the same time.

That's the thing. So gorged on historical import, it is hard to tell if familiarity drains or heightens the impact of actually being in this lushly polished, wood-paneled room. There is no doubt a name for this psychological phenomenon, but don't ask me what it is. Everything seems more real in the photographs, on display steps away from the actual courtroom, in the adjacent exhibit.

Unlike the self-loving Göring (one of the Reich's more prominent morphine fiends, along with Herr Schicklgruber), none of the others—in accounts and photographs—come off so insanely arrogant. None, in these group prisoner photos and videos at the museum (and of course it's a museum—is there a murderous regime or torture plant that has not fast-forwarded to an "educational center"?), look as nervous as Rudolf Hess. Fresh from the shame of being plucked out of British prison after fleeing for Scotland in a stolen plane at the height of the war, Hess looks positively Elisha Cook–like, a put-upon little man who, if he didn't suffer twitches, might as well have. He has the cringing mien of a man about to be slapped by a woman named Baby. Perhaps it is true that he and Hitler were secret snuggle-buddies, and he misses his man. Love!

Like Albert Speer, Hess had the good sense to apologize, and got off with life instead of the rope. Speer one-upped the mea culpa, taking personal responsibility for his country's crimes and the hundreds of thousands of slave laborers who worked in his name. He was given twenty years in prison. Got out in 1966. Died in '81. Long enough to hear the Sex Pistols, in swastika armbands, sing "Belsen Was a Gas"; not long enough to see GG Allin take an onstage dump while wearing a lurid führer mustache. (Regarding the Sex Pistols, what *would* the expired Nazis have made of the lyrics to that catchy number? "*Belsen was a gas I heard the other day / In the open graves where the Jews all lay / Life is fun and I wish you were here / They wrote on postcards to those held dear.*" I imagine Julius Streicher would have loved it. Hess would have probably scratched his head. And Göring, that party animal, might have tapped his gout-swollen toes.)

But listen. After learning, in the first twenty minutes, that only ten Nazi heavies sentenced at Nuremberg were hanged, and few even received life, I feel a disquiet that makes me want to punch walls and tune out all other details. Maybe, progressive that I am, I do oppose the death penalty. But hey . . . tell me you wouldn't smother Hitler in his diapers if you had the chance. And all the defendants were some version of Hitler. Or wanted to be. Hitler spinoffs.

Each of the Allies, it says on a wall plaque, sent judges

to Nuremberg to try the monsters. Though not all their leaders were thrilled about it. Churchill considered the Axis bigwigs outlaws and wanted to shoot them out of hand. Stalin, being Stalin, wanted to round up fifty thousand Nazis and go Stalin on them. The French—who shouldn't have been there, given they turned over tons of Jews, and folded immediately—had an opinion no one cares about. But the Americans, in an early incarnation of They Go Low, We Go High, decided they wanted to show the world that a civilized nation doesn't traffic in vengeance.[1]

Unless, of course, it does, and I have things completely wrong, and there's a secret history in which Americans were as brutal as the rest.

(In the hours I spend visiting the site of the Nuremberg trials, I find myself daydreaming about W in the dock where Eichmann sat, answering for Iraq, and all *that* horror—which no one talks about anymore—right up to the generations of deformed and brain-fucked depleted-uranium babies who live in the hellhole America left behind by way of spreading democracy. Politics and history have more meat on their bones when you're tromping around on the bones they crushed.)

As I write this, I can't recall, for the life of me, if the Palace of Justice gave tourists free reign of the court; if I ambled under a velvet rope, or bribed a guard, or if I'm dreaming all of this. But I seem to recall sitting down, getting up, and

---

1. And then there's the oddball case of Admiral Karl Dönitz, head of the German Navy, indicted for giving orders not to help survivors of sinking ships in the Atlantic. Which might have, as they say, held more water if the USA had not issued identical orders in the Pacific, in the war with Japan. How, asked Dönitz's German lawyer, could Germany be punished for a crime America also committed? And so Dönitz dodged the noose, living on until 1980.

sitting down again; bouncing from chair to chair where Göring, Rudolph Hess, Foreign Minister von Ribbentrop, Field Marshal Keitel, and those other *machers* parked their carcasses. Among them—my personal obsession—aforementioned publisher Julius Streicher, a bullwhip-carrying sadist who would feel right at home today, in twenty-first-century Proud Boy–land. Streicher, call him a bigot visionary, was father of the fat, big-nosed, fräulein-violating, shekel-dripping Jew caricatures you could find, then, in *Der Stürmer*, and today on *Reddit*, *Daily Stormer*, or countless other venues here in White Nationalist America.

We know (today) that two weeks after their trial, all the men, minus Hess, were destined for a quick death by hanging. And that the hangman, a short fireplug of a man, Master Sergeant John C. Woods of San Antonio, had ideas of his own.

Did Woods, history asks, deliberately botch the hangings? So that instead of instantly dying—*snap!*—of a broken neck, Herrs von Ribbentrop, Keitel, Streicher, and the rest were left to dangle after the trapdoor opened, swinging back and forth in the brightly lit gymnasium, where they'd built the gallows. Succumbing to slow, agonizing strangulation.

(The worst botched death story I know involves a guy I heard about at San Quentin who—if I have this right—tried to shoot himself after accidentally killing his only child, and instead succeeded in blowing the bottom third of his face off, leaving him a sideshow act, part normal-faced, part skeleton with dentures, for which—this is the heartbreaker—he was busted for weapons possession—his third strike—and sent away for life. A story worth recalling, for all you gratitude seekers. Whatever hell you think you're going through, at least it's not *that*.)

Okay then. Von Ribbentrop, first on the bill, took fourteen minutes to die; Keitel choked for almost half an hour. And so on. While this had the (admittedly inhumane) effect of torturing the prisoners to death, it also had the (admittedly inhumane) effect of giving them the chance to speechify before the drop. Ranging from von Ribbentrop, who climbed the thirteen steps to the gallows, took fourteen minutes to choke, and, like every Miss America ever crowned, expressed his wish for world peace; to madman Streicher, who hung in for twenty-four minutes, plenty of time to babble about the Thousand-Year Reich before going out with the evergreen *Heil Hitler!*

Mind you, we've strayed a bit from Holocaust bussing. But in the interest of plumbing the weirder fallout of genocide justice, let me just say that bad hangman Woods, still in the army, was stationed in a Pacific atoll years later, in 1950, along with some of our new German friends, thanks to Operation Paperclip, which saw America embracing usefully talented Nazis to help with our nuclear pursuits. Somehow, the ex–Hitler ecstatics found out that Woods was on the island. Whereupon, mysteriously, the notorious Nazi-roper was electrocuted while changing light bulbs in a pool of water. Rumor had it, at the time, that our new Nazi friends clocked the executioner, found out where he was, and exacted vengeance for their badly hanged Third Reich brethren. History within history. Or, to paraphrase Susan Sontag, whatever you think is happening is not what's happening.

Now back to our main event. Auf Wiedersehen, Nuremberg; hallo, Dachau.

I made the decision, after my Bud Cort/*Triumph of the Will* fiasco, not to bust out the one cultural reference to Dachau I ever listened to on acid while eating Mallomars and laugh-crying as a teenager: Captain Beefheart's "Dachau Blues." Due to a scratch in the album, *Trout Mask Replica*, the song repeated endlessly. But the acid kept anyone from getting off the couch and changing it, so the lyrics are permanently burned in my brainpan. I can still hear them, and find myself belting them out at odd, inappropriate times. Though when, really, *is* Beefheart's Dachau appropriate, if not now, on a bus full of travelers bound for the camp itself?

Reason prevails. I restrain myself and only sing the ditty in my head (though I think my lips are moving): *Dachau Blues, those poor Jews / Still cryin' 'bout the burnin' back in World War II's / One mad man, six million lose / Down in Dachau blues, Down in Dachau blues . . .*

You get the gist. Aside from that fact that I'd probably be hurled headlong into a Bavarian manhole for trying, there's no imitating Beefheart's four-and-a-half-octave range. Which gives the song the disturbing beauty of a sea chantey sung by a meat grinder, in a cave.

In addition to Beefheart, Dachau had another pop culture moment that comes to mind. One (I still can't explain it) that I recall at exactly the same moment my eyes meet Tad's and he shoots me a knowing wink.

"*Family Guy*, right?"

Color me gobsmacked. "How did you—?"

Tad grins in the way you'd expect a big-jawed fella in

madras shorts from Texas would grin. "Figured you for a *Family Guy* fan" is his guileless explanation. Though for the remainder of the trip, mind already warped by sleeplessness, I semi-believe Tad can read my thoughts, especially the deeply wrong ones, and try to aim my forehead away whenever I see him staring. Depression, paranoia, and—why mince words?—impaired judgment can blend to a fine froth that washes over the brain, marinating every belief to grievance, morphing every uttered word to an assault in disguise. Everywhere, to steal a line from poet Michael Ryan, "threats instead of trees . . ."

The *Family Guy* episode in question features a despondent cow in a McBurgertown slaughterhouse. For sheer yuks, Tad leans over the back of his seat and recites the cow's line, doing his best Ricardo Montalbán: "'In here we call it Dachau . . . except we spell the *chau* part c-o-w, like *cow*, so it's kind of a dark joke.'"

His Ricardo Montalbán is so spot-on I'm a little alarmed. I wrote the guy off as a Lone Star suburbo jim-jim, and he turns out to be the Rich Little of West Texas.

"I love," Tad continues, "when the dog goes, 'Yeah, it's a Holocaust joke. That's really funny.' I mean, the dog's so *dry!*" Just recounting it, he cracks up all over again.

Luckily, before Tad tells me he bought Seth MacFarlane's album—*In Full Swing*—where *Family Guy*'s creator croons Sinatra-esque standards, Suzannah cuts in with what I've come to recognize as her sour smile, in an unmistakably disapproving tone: "I'm not sure I always understand American comedians."

"Oh, it's not a comedian. *Family Guy*'s an animated show," Tad explains, and turns to me. "Really good, right?"

I respond with what I hope is the world's smallest nod, caught between backing up my bus buddy and seeming like a total lame to the woman in charge.

Again.

# CHAPTER 22
## *DACHAU BLUES*

🚌 🚌 🚌

BY THE TIME WE GET TO DACHAU on day eleven, I feel like going to concentration camps is my job. I get on the bus in the morning and go to work. You'd think this would make a person jaded. But what it makes me is more attentive to the particulars of horror, a reluctant, de facto connoisseur of murderous specifics. Which leads us to the Dachau crematorium. And forgive the abrupt transition; the niceties of narrative crumble in the face of accumulated detail. The little things that make the big thing real. Or realer. Everybody's seen the bodies, the pits, the gaunt and dead-eyed victims. But what about the ceiling hooks in the crematorium at Dachau?

Think of it: the SS hanged victims in front of the ovens so they could see what was coming. As far as I know, this was the only camp where victims weren't dead before they got to the flames. Instead, at Dachau you saw your immediate future—the final performance in which you were obliged to participate, for an audience of death workers. Even more hellish to contemplate—and of course we can't stop—before the hangings commenced, it was someone's job to stand on a ladder, drill holes over his head, and screw those hooks into the ceiling. The Dachau super.

There are two theories about those hangings: the pragmatic and the sadistic. Either the Germans were low on bullets or, my personal belief, the SS were driven to ever more savagery to torment the doomed before they were allowed to die, if only to entertain themselves.

The noose, tied to the hook, was slipped around the victim's neck as they faced the flaming maw. As at Auschwitz, extending from the ovens is a sliding tray, those long handles on the end for the Sonderkommandos to grab and shove the newly dead into the fire. A sign on the wall tells visitors, "Each of the four furnaces could cremate two to three corpses at once. The ovens were connected to the chimney by an underground canal."

Ten steps from rope to inferno.

Toward the end, before Allies liberated the place, there was not enough coal to fire the ovens. In photos, you can see how the stick-thin corpses were left outside the crematorium, or stacked within, spilling out the doors. (Is that, one wonders, what the late Lou Reed meant, in "Heroin" by "all the dead bodies piled up mounds"? Was he singing of his murdered forefathers? Or just New York in the seventies?)

Speaking of . . . acccording to the *New York Times*, Lou described his look in that era as the "Dachau panda"—chopped-short peroxide hair and heavy black circles painted under his eyes. That's the second rock song I've squeezed into the Dachau section, and I'm not sure why. Unless it's that right now, as when this was actually happening, I'm as sleep-deprived as a speed freak on a ten-day run. Minus the crank and dental issues. (Actually, hold the dental issues. I've got the kind of teeth, when I go to the dentists, the dental assistants can't help themselves and flat-out ask, "How can you live this way?" Lots of unsightly incisors and gaps, a shade that varies from battleship gray to banana yellow, but not enough gold to interest an enterprising Nazi. Saving up!)

I'm so tired, I'm not even going to try to tease meaning out of the fact that there's a Finnish punk band, Dachau; an Irish punk rocker, Deko Dachau (lead singer of Dublin's Paranoid Visions); and too many titles like the Underdogs' "East of Dachau" to cram into a paragraph. What can you say, but there's just something about Dachau? No one, as far as I can tell, has hopped on board with Billy Auschwitz. (You can almost imagine the review in *NME:* "A little Neil Diamond, a little drain cleaner.") Ditto Betty Buchenwald, or Sluts of Sachsenhausen. Nothing packs the punch of Dachau. The Sid Vicious number "Belsen Was a Gas" being the exception that proves the rule. It was so easy to shock back then, the whole enterprise seems quaint.

But I'm exaggerating about the sleep thing. These days, reconstructing memories, I snag about an hour a night, usually the four-to-five shift, then bolt awake to the clutter of Nazi photos, Nazi books, and Nazi videos that spill out of every room in my house. The Reich-merch that will make me look like a full-on *Daily Stormer* fan if I keel over and the paramedics show up. Depending on their bent, the ambulance jockeys will either give me extras or skip the life-saving maneuvers altogether and drop me down the stairs. Ours is a divided country.

The sight and stench of corpses, according to Dachau's

American liberators, induced vomiting, trauma, and rage among the locals. Call it the dead's revenge upon the living. As at Buchenwald, the US forced townsfolk and Nazi Party members to come to the camp and help dispose of corpses. As at Buchenwald, they were shocked. They had *no idea*.

And once again, your author faces the very uncomfortable, ever-unavoidable truth that the subject he's describing has been described elsewhere, and better, much better, a million times.

What can you do?

Here, ladies and gentleman of the jury, I am going to take a break, to pursue a question—no doubt frivolous, relatively—that I've been meaning to look into before I even set foot in Auschwitz. What exactly do the different colors of the prisoners' badges actually signify? Like I said, frivolous. But still . . . In my twenties I lived on Hudson, near Christopher Street, in New York City, and it took most of the summer to suss out what the back-pocket hankies worn by neighborhood gents strolling the sidewalk were meant to convey. Not to compare deciphering ass hankies with camp badges—just that deciphering (decipherization?) is one more window into the culture that generated them.

But handkerchiefs, it hardly needs mentioning, were voluntary; camp badges exactly the opposite. Yellow, in the West Village, conveyed a penchant for water sports. (The Steele dossier could have come wrapped in a yellow hanky.) In the camps, yellow meant Jew. Pink meant homosexual. Violet was for Jehovah's Witnesses. Red, political prisoners—the first victims who had the misfortune to be thrown in the camps.

To my surprise, I heard a South African guide I hadn't paid, just glommed onto, explain that Germans weren't even the first to assign yellow to Jews. The practice—not so fun fact—originated with Muslims. Around 807 AD, during the reign of a caliph named Harun al-Rashid, Baghdad Jews were made known with yellow fringes. Not long after, under Caliph al-Mutawakkil (AD 847–861), Jews were forced to sport a patch shaped like a donkey, while their Christian brethren were relegated ones that were swine-shaped. Egyptian Jews were commanded to wear bells. Interesting too—if wholly irrelevant—in Caravaggio's sixteenth-century paintings, the artist used yellow shawls to mark women as prostitutes. But back to the story at hand.

Before the pre-Nazi badge and bell ordinances, explained the South African, there was a category of prisoner I'd never expected: the stupid.

That's right. These unfortunates wore badges marked *Blöd* (German for "stupid"). The thing I could not glean, info-mooching off the young Johannesburger (who, to my relief, did not seem to mind me tapping into his spiel), was what exactly comprised criminal stupidity? Idiocy worthy of detention in a KZ (KZ, I learned—way too late—being the preferred contemporary term for concentration camp). I could find no reference to the *Blöd* prisoners in any postbus research. But it's an intriguing idea. If the state, in America, took to criminalizing morons, then who knows who would be left—in or out of government? On the other hand, why ask?

If those who wrote about the camps had to wear badges, then along with my yellow Jew signifier, I'm guessing I'd be slapped with a *Blöd* badge too. There's a certain arro-

gance in thinking you can say anything new about a subject so beautifully, deeply, and heartbreakingly chronicled
by others. Which is why, he wrote defensively, all I've tried
to do is focus on my own reactions—the what-it's-like of it
all. The fact is that it's not about facts so much as the experience of facing them, staring at them, standing where the
flesh-and-blood outrages occurred before time and history withered them, as they inevitably do, into statistics.
By now, I catch myself typing, "I am getting burned out on
concentration camps." And hate myself all over the place.
(Last night I dreamed that a pile of naked bodies, with
the horrific, elongated El Greco quality that starvation,
death, and careless disposal creates, somehow appeared
in my driveway, and I had to make my way through them
to get to my car, wrestling with the question of whether I
should stop and "do something" about the corpses, or just
move a few so I could back out and head to Trader Joe's for
senior-dog dog food. Delmore Schwartz famously wrote,
"In dreams begin responsibilities." What I'm responsible
for, after dreaming of driveway death camp corpses, in the
context of kibble, is a question I've yet to answer.

I don't know what nonstop, day-in-and-day-out exposure to this subject does to a person, except perhaps to
keep the eternal flame of rage and determination burning inside them. I can't pretend to grasp those depths. But
more and more I've got a sort of baffled, bone-deep admi-
ration for the individuals who labor, say, at Vad Yashem,
or any of the extermination camp museums, those who
daily subject themselves to the unrelenting *This really
happened*-ness that photos, films, and the rest of the evidence forever assert, the thousands whose life's work,

on the ground, is keeping the greatest crime scene of the twentieth century forever alive.

From a lot of angles, these are the heroes. (And I'm including you, surly Auschwitz men's room attendant.)

An interesting feature of the Dachau display is a twenty-two-minute film, taking Holocaust newbies and veterans alike from the beginnings of Nazism all the way through the liberation of the camps. Footage is gruesome, but the sprinkling of kids young enough, technically, to qualify it as strictly PG-13 viewing do not seem to mind. Nor do their parents. I'm guessing, most homes have the History and Military channels—or some version thereof— which run enough, pardon the expression, boiler-plate concentration camp footage to jade most viewers by the time they're sixteen. The corpse mountains may be horrifying, but never unfamiliar.

The theater is airy, anything but glum. Viewers sit in long rows, with—at least the day I was there—room enough for social distancing long before it was necessary. The German version—well, not the German version, the German-language version, runs at 9:30, 11, 1:30, 2:30, and 3:30. Whether or not there is a German version, editori-ally different from the English offering (at 10, 11:30, 12:30, 2, and 3), I do not stay around to find out. Not that it mat-ters. I don't speak much German. But I know enough to spot "Wir hätten gewinnen sollen!" (We should have won!) or "Hitler lebt!" (Hitler lives!) if it's stamped across the screen in a flashing chyron. In a surprising (or not) slap in the face to Italian and French visitors, management has seen fit to slate just one showing of the movie in those langauges. Read into it what you will.

# CHAPTER 23
## WITH APOLOGIES TO MS. THORNE

🚌 🚌 🚌

IN JANUARY 2020, WHILE AT WORK on this book, I found out that Dyanne Thorne, the actress who played Ilse in *Ilsa, She Wolf of the SS*, had passed on at the ripe old age of eighty-three. The *Hollywood Reporter*, in its obit, quotes the actress reminiscing about one of the more grisly and most famous scenes from the movie, wherein Ilse removes the male equipment from one of the many men she takes from the ranks of Buchenwald prisoners. "This was the sweetest actor in the world that they castrated. I must tell you, that was probably the most shocking scene in my entire life."

As it happens, Ms. Thorne and I crossed paths many years ago, when my writing partner at the time, director Stephen Sayadian (AKA Rinse Dream) was casting one of the leads in our remake of *Dr. Caligari*. (Crying out to be done!) On that occasion, like a couple of fanboys, we peppered Ms. Thorne with questions about her *She Wolf* experience. (How often do you get to talk to a legend?) Surprisingly, or not, Ms. Thorne—whom we did not cast (a case, I'm ashamed to admit, of blatant ageism)—was mum on the subject of her most famous role. The woman was famous for a thing she was not particularly proud of.

A situation to which I could, in my own small way, relate. Having chronicled, in an earlier book, my extremely brief time scribbling on *ALF* while smashed on heroin—a situation that made its way into a movie—I found myself, by way of cosmic joke, forever linked with the alien puppet. Even (private-island money!) credited as its creator. When, for example, a mutual friend, progressive activist Jane Hamsher (who produced said movie, *Permanent Midnight*, after *Natural Born Killers*), brought me up to a journalist I admire, Matt Taibbi, Matt's reaction, as she related it, was wholly typical: "Oh yeah, the *ALF* guy . . ."

Thank you, sir. May I have another?

So RIP, Ms. Thorne, who I will not refer to as "Ilsa." (And I'm sure there's a reason for the filmmaker's switch from the authentic "Ilse" to the fictional "Ilsa." No doubt the families of celebrity sadists are as litigious as families of non-sadist celebs.) Instead, let's remember her in her final incarnation as a nondenominational reverend and wedding officiator in Las Vegas. Though even here, the actress could not completely escape her most celebrated role. All, no doubt, in good fun, she presided over nuptials referred to as "Ilsa weddings"—because who wouldn't want an Ilsa wedding? With—as the *Hollywood Reporter* explained in her obit—"the swastika replaced by an American flag." Take that, Nazi scum!

To the end, apparently, the illustrious actress was a tad surprised by the movie for which she was justly renowned. Had she, by chance, read the aforementioned Susan Sontag essay, "Fascinating Fascism"—which came out the same year as *Ilsa*, 1975, in the *New York Review of Books*—she might have understood the film's lasting (if disturbing) appeal. Listen: "Right-wing movements, however puritanical and repressive the realities they usher in, have an erotic surface . . ." What people forget—or never knew—is that Israel itself, in 1963, when half its population were Holocaust survivors, had to pass a law banning porny Nazi prisoner–themed comics, known as "stalags." The books were so popular, according to a Hebrew University survey, they comprised "top reading material for eighteen-year-old Israeli boys."

Unlike *Ilsa*, which you can sniff out on VHS if you really dig, should you want to read a snatch of *I Was Colonel Schultz's Private Bitch*—the all-time best-selling stalag—you'll need to fly to the Holy Land, visit the National Library in Jerusalem, secure permission from the librarian, and head down to the basement where they keep the hard stuff.

# CHAPTER 24
## *STANLEY MANLY*

🚌 🚌 🚌

AT BREAKFAST, ON DACHAU DAY, Bulldozer Bob pops over and sits down on my table, already chatting at me.

"Oooh, look at Stanley Manly. You do push-ups every morning?"

"What?"

I am so distracted by events domestic and professional, along with the whole World War II Genocide smorgasbord, I answer Bob without even thinking how he might have known of my hotel room health regimen. One that consists mainly of hurling myself on the floor and doing push-ups upon awakening, to keep myself from pounding my head off the wall. Which, by the way, Sofitel can actually bill you for, if you leave a hole. It's listed on your bill as "Miscellaneous."

Two months ago, I had to move out fast from a house in Pasadena, a rental I'd fled to after selling a home in LA I'd owned for a dozen years—long story—and had to explain to the realtor, during the pre-lease-breaking corporate-landlord tour—why there were so many holes in the plaster walls. All in odd, or seemingly odd, places. Like beneath the banister, halfway down the scuffed-by-the-decades black wooden stairs, above the toilet (upstairs and down)—more of a punch than a headbang—even in the garage, between the light switch and the shelf full of ventriloquism books (how-tos and memoirs, including one called *Sing, Laugh, and Gargle*, which I wish to fuck I'd lifted, and can find nowhere on the Internet or the Satan that is Amazon). I don't know much about the previous tenants, but it's somehow good to know that at least one of them could talk out of a dummy. My three-year-old would be impressed.

The Pasadena house was built in 1929. At some point, the basement, banked by dirt on three sides, with a carpet of rat droppings, was divided into a warren of tiny rooms, three with no windows. I was told by the nice Armenian lady across the street, who said she'd lived there for forty-two years, that in the eighties the landlords rented the place out to Chinese students, attendees of the community college around the corner.

Given that the rooms were sub-tiny, that each was affixed with small iron rings in the corner of the floor, I couldn't help but wonder if there was some kind of servitude going on. If, at some point in the not-too-distant past, a team of bread-and-water-fed unfortunates were stuck in the cellar assembling cheap toys or stuffing throw pillows. It's a grim thought, and when I asked the realty company, they denied everything. (And seemed deeply creeped out that I'd asked.) "We don't know what goes on in our houses, we can't," the woman at the other end informed me. "We assume what the tenants are doing is just living there." Unless—the *other* explanation—there had been a full-on dom or domme keeping his/her/their subs in their places, providing the restraint and humiliation the subterranean pain-and-shame seekers so deeply craved, right there in the bowels of Rose Bowl Parade–land. Whether a for-profit or "lifestyle" situation, I guess we'll never know. None of the neighbors—including my elderly Armenian acquaintance—were talking.

But back to my own lifestyle—is depression a lifestyle?— how do you explain that you put your head through the walls? Or—is this less incriminating?—punched them? Blowing off steam. Do you just toss it out there, ready to field questions? *Let me get this straight, Mr. Stahl, you put gashes in the plaster, and you don't repair them? You just leave them there?* Or do you plead ignorance—*That's so weird, I've never noticed those holes before!*—and blanket deny any mental health–related explanations. (When it comes to mental health, in my experience, blankets are often involved.)

As it happens, my father was a plaster smasher, and by the time he died, our own house in Pittsburgh, as I've probably babbled elsewhere, had been transformed into a museum of Dad rage. We could have had little plaques— like the ones by the torture rooms at Dachau—with the date of every cranial assault. *Thanksgiving 1967, argument over stuffing. Too dry!*

In the end, the property people just charged me for the drywall. I think the woman may have felt bad for me, or perhaps had a headbanger of her own in the family. We're not that rare. Mental illness was a plague *before* the plague.

I believe the realtor rep's name was Mrs. Fettermagen. (It's German; loose translation, *jumbo gut*.) And to this day, after watching Frau F. study the boxes and shelves of Nazi death camp lore during the Creepy Tenant Damage Tour, I could not say if her expression was approving, wistful, horrified, or something else I hadn't thought of. Whatever, she said the plaster mishaps could be covered by the deposit, then asked if I was some kind of writer. And when I said yes, she asked a follow-up: "In English or German?" I wasn't sure what she was implying, and burst out, "English, but there are German editions!"

Which I don't know why I said, except that I wasn't sure if she maybe wanted me to be a Nazi. How do you ask?

After visiting Germany, and seeing the faces of very old citizens, I still can't shake the sense that they were all Nazis, and maybe now, in the FAB—Fascists Are Back!—era, I can finally come out of the closet and own it. The question is whether Mrs. Large Gut (a slender woman) thought I was, or wasn't, German, and what she thought being a German actually implied. (Did Jews, in the twenties, ever call each other paranoid, before what happened happened? Was Kafka nervous?)

For one bad second, looking back, I wonder if Bulldozer Bob's spying has some Jew-hating dimension. But how would that manifest as physical fitness mockery? He wouldn't be ridiculing my post-push-up carpet collapse, he'd be making fun of my bacon avoidance, or Jewy neuroses. My Jew-rosis.

Anyway, like I say, it was more than a little weird when, after inviting himself over for brekky, Bob put down his sausage and said, "You look quite good with your shirt off." Maybe it's that *quite* that did it. Or maybe the fact that, given my penchant for instantly closing all drapes and shutters the second I set foot in a hotel, I had no idea how Bob could possibly have seen me unless he peeked through a keyhole.

Can you peek through keyholes when the key is a plastic card?

No doubt, I tell myself, the whole shirt-off thing is some strain of Aussie bro-bonding. I try not to react. Though I notice Douglas, sitting a foot or two away, raise an eyebrow in my direction. He actually snickers. "A peeping Tom in our midst! Oh Tito, we had better close the windows. Bob likes looking at handsome men. Be careful, Gerald!"

"Whoa!" I hear myself say.

"Germany," Douglas exclaims, "land of party sausage!"

"Party sausage?"

Tito rolls his eyes. "Oh come on, Papi, you know Hitler was a big old queen." When I admit that no, in fact, I did not know that, Tito, who is slightly hard of hearing, bellows, "Hell-*OOOO!* Adolf Hitler was a total power bottom!"

Douglas mistakes my alarm for surprise. "Someone's a little slow on the uptake. Why do you think Auntie Adolf had to murder the Brownshirts? In World War I, he had a boytoy in the trenches. Everybody knew. The head of the storm troopers, Ernst Röhm—who was out and proud—was totally blackmailing him."

"Can you say Night of the Long Knives?" Tito adds, volume only slightly lower. "Of course the sissies had to be killed."

"Wow," I say, "this is . . . I mean, this is—"

"This is *what?*" Doug interrupts. "Don't tell me you didn't know Hitler was bent. Please! The man wanted to be beat, kicked, and pooped on. What that poor Eva had to go through! Did you know—?"

"No!" I say, before someone from the Munich Morals Squad can swoop in. A family at the next table looks aghast. "I mean, I didn't know you were such history buffs."

"Buff shmuff," Douglas says, "we're insomniacs. Between the History Channel and the Military Channel, it's all Nazi all the time."

"We could probably give a Ned Talk," Tito says

"It's TED," Doug corrects.

Tito looks around. "Where?"

There follows a moment of uncomfortable silence, before Bulldozer Bob pipes up. "Pooped on? Yeah, nah." Clearly, all this gay Hitler stuff is getting to him. "Yeah, nah," he repeats.

Douglas looks concerned. "You okay there, Bob?"

"Yeah, nah."

"I think we've made Bob nervous," Douglas says to his partner. And then, to Bob, "Sorry about that. Sometimes we get carried away."

Bob just nods.

"Pardon the digression," Doug says. "What were we talking about, you know, before we got inappropriate? Oh right—are you a peeper, Bob?"

"Okay, come on, guys!" I can't stand seeing Bob so embarrassed. "If you're stuck in a bus all day, you have to do something, right?"

"Of course you do," Douglas responds, his tone risqué as a cocktail napkin.

Suddenly Tito starts in singing: *"Jeepers creepers, where'd ya get those peepers?"*

"I wasn't peeping!" protests Bulldozer.

With impeccable timing, Suzannah shows up and takes the four of us in with a knowing eye. "I think we should probably go," she says, and lowers her voice conspiratorially. "We've had complaints."

Bob grabs his stein and knocks back the last of his dunkel. "Yeah, nah," he says. "I'm having a bad day."

# CHAPTER 25
## STEPPING ON THE FACES OF THE DEAD

🚌 🚌 🚌

BY THE TIME I GOT TO DACHAU I was almost sleepwalking, unable to give the exhibitions the attention they deserve. It was a long day before even getting to those crematorium hooks. After the Dachau movie, I strolled into the exhibition hall, which had much more high-tech museum gear than either Buchenwald or Auschwitz. With touch screen photographs suspended from the ceiling, you could place a finger on the display and be taken into some colorful, creative discursion on the subject at hand. I won't spend time describing the different sections. The touch screens, most of which actually worked, struck me as a distracting novelty, at uncomfortable odds with the place itself. Though they absolutely enhanced the experience, they made it more slick. I don't want my Holocaust display slick. Give me the Auschwitz treatment: a giant pile of hair behind a pane of glass.

I could not tell you why, but the impact of any given subject seems to decrease in direct proportion to how cutting edge the system is that delivers it. Calling Reich-Marshall McLuhan! In the corridors at Auschwitz, they put up old-fashioned framed photographs and thumbnail bios of the actual inmates. It's the same lo-fi technology as the *Most Wanted* posters in the US Post Office. (Also high-impact.) Photos and bios are presented the same way in the Auschwitz Memorial Twitter feed. Of which, let it be said, I am a huge fan. (If "fan" is the right word; and now that I'm looking at it, it definitely isn't. Apologies. The last thing I want is to get in a Twitter war with Auschwitz.) The point is, this is one case where the technology would seem to be perfect. What's more, there's good reason the museum should give victims their own Twitter feed: the dead can't tweet. And they deserve to be represented. Happily, until Jack Dorsey nails down the beyond-the-grave market, the Memorial has it covered.

I find myself by the block devoted to "medical experimentation." As I linger, I am struck by an image, as if injected into my brain, of something that went on, a mere seven decades ago, not inside these chambers, but right outside. Quite possibly, on the spot I am occupying now.

Imagine, in the dead of Bavarian winter, a tub on the ground filled with freezing water, into which naked prisoners were submerged, forcibly held under, whereupon the "doctors" on hand tried, with varying methods—and varying degrees of success—to revive them. For the Nazis, these freezing, fatal plunges were more than mere acts of sadism. There was, you know, a *reason*. Courtesy of the RAF, which was picking apart Hermann Göring's Luftwaffe over the North Atlantic, more and more pilots had been plunging out of the firmament into the frigid waters of the North Sea. Steps had to be taken. Titled, by the literalists in charge, "The Treatment of Shock from Prolonged Exposure to Cold, Especially in Water," the thrust of the

Dachau hypothermia experiments—run by one Sigmund Rascher—was to discover the most efficacious way to revive aviators once they'd made the involuntary dive into the Atlantic.

Among the discoveries brought to the world by Dr. Rascher was that it took between eighty minutes to six hours for freezing water to kill naked victims—whereas clothed men died after six to seven hours. (That the odds of a pilot leaping naked from their plane prior to a crash—or removing their clothes, inside the plane, before impact—were zero to nil, does not seem to have factored into Rascher's dogged pursuit of the truth. This was science for science's sake! A second big query, for the doctor, was whether what did kill the unfortunate subjects of the experiment was cardiac or respiratory arrest. Subject of lively debate by German thermal-torment pros at the time.)

With Himmler's aid, we learn, Rascher thwarted repeated attempts by the medical establishment of the military to influence, participate in, or wrest control of the project. Meaning, essentially, that Himmler wanted to make sure hypothermia remained his and Rascher's own little party.

So okay then! As at Buchenwald and Auschwitz, the grotesque charade of "medical experiments" at Dachau was used to torture prisoners in ever more arcane and diabolical fashion. Among other notions, it was Sigmund Rascher's idea, by way of warming up the freezing subjects, to take them out of the ice-cold vats and toss them into boiling water. Surprisingly—to no one, ever—this technique did not work. Another of Rascher's ideas was to enlist the aid of prostitutes, often Romani ladies plucked from the women's concentration camp at Ravensbrück. The doctor's idea was to press the poor, unconscious individual's body between the females for a slow "body massage." This last, for reasons we can probably surmise, was so appealing to Rascher, he brought in Himmler to observe the proceedings. Who said Nazis couldn't let their hair down?

All of which would be no more than par for the course, in Nazi nightmare medicine, were it not for the fact that, fast-forward half a century or so—up to 1988—and American Robert Pozos, director of the hypothermia research laboratory at the University of Minnesota, Duluth, decided it might be worthwhile to dig up Rascher's catchily titled old study—"The Treatment of Shock from Prolonged, etc."—to see if the long-dead torture-meisters had discovered anything applicable to modern studies in the field.

Hard to believe, but true. It must be. It's all there in the *New York Times*, May 12, 1988. Listen: "[B]ecause mammals differ widely in their physiological response to cold, hypothermia research is uniquely dependent on human test subjects. Of the Dachau experiment, Pozos said, 'It could advance my work in that it takes human subjects farther than we're willing.'"

Dr. Franz Blaha supplies a chilling coda to events in a remarkable collection edited by John Carey and published in 1987, *Eyewitness to History*: "About three hundred persons were used in these experiments. The majority died. Of those who lived, many became mentally deranged . . . Those not killed were sent to invalid blocks and were killed. I only know two who survived, a Yugoslav and a Pole. And both became mental cases."

Strangely, in his plea for furthering his own niche of medical science on the backs of dead Dachau inmates, Dr. Pozos left out the fact that Sigmund Rascher, the main scientist behind those Nazi hypothermia studies (whose studies he was resurrecting) had a few glaringly bizarre data points of his own. Beginning with the peculiar relationship between Doc Rascher and SS overlord Reichsführer Himmler. Rascher, who was held in low esteem by fellow Nazi medicos, had married Himmler's former mistress (fifteen years his elder), apparently taking the ex-cabaret singer off Himmler's hands in return for a plum medical position at Dachau. The marriage appears to have been his primary qualification for the job.

Himmler was obsessed with increasing the fertility of good German stock, thereby ensuring the sturdy future of the Reich. By way of further ingratiating himself to Uncle Heinrich, Rascher claimed to have invented a way to extend the childbearing years of the noble German hausfrau. As proof he offered his own wife, whom Rascher claimed had given birth to three children in quick succession—after turning forty-eight. Unfortunately for Dr. Rascher, during the missus's remarkable fourth pregnancy, she was arrested for trying to kidnap an infant. Whereupon it was discovered that all three of her "miracle" late-life babies had been abducted or bought. And if this bit of scientific fraud wasn't damning enough, there was the little matter of Rascher's personal hobbies, as described in a 1990 *New England Journal of Medicine* article on the subject: "Rascher collected human skin for making saddles, riding breeches, and"—paging Ilse Koch—"ladies' handbags."

Eventually—sometimes there *are* happy endings!—

Rascher's scientific fraud got him in hot water of his own, and he ended up with the rare fate of being executed, on Himmler's orders, at the same concentration camp where he'd operated for the previous three years.

Anyway, I realize I've been just standing here, muttering to myself and imagining prisoners dragged out and dunked in vats of freezing liquid for the benefit of mankind—or at least Heinrich Himmler, who liked to perv on icy three-ways. Time to move on. There is, if you're prone to such things, not a single spot in any camp where one couldn't stand, imagining this *this-really-happened* scenario or that, and let the repulsion and shock at what happened freeze you right there.

At some point, in the land of Holocaust, contempla-tion turns to paralysis, and you end up going nowhere, gripped by the moral equivalent of couch lock. Staring into the abyss until it doesn't just stare back, it reaches up and grabs you by the larynx, and you find yourself staring out, not in . . . and then what? You go numb or you wish you could. But enough about me. Beckett couldn't go on, and went on. He also drove André the Giant to school; separate issue. Young André—since we're on the subject—was 240 pounds and six foot three at twelve, too big for the school bus, and Mr. Beckett, the friendly neighbor, was happy to help. André—real name André René Rous-simoff—was also a Jew. In France. Had he been born in '36 instead of '46, he might have ended up in the back of a freight car instead of an existential Peugeot. Hard not to imagine the kind of experiments Nazi "scientists" might have done on André. My guess is, some Mengele—or

Rascher—would have tried to isolate his acromegaly gene, to try to breed giant Germans . . .

Thankfully, my mind stops grinding when I catch sight of Shlomo, staring off in his own muttering fog fifty feet away. The camps, I've noticed, are full of people staring off, gripped by their own private revelations, and I find myself stepping respectfully around them, as you would a sadhu in Calcutta, giving them the space they need for reflection or meditation.

Dachau's barracks have been demolished, but their rectangular outlines are marked on the ground, in row after row, creating zones of designated absence that, curiously, imbue the empty spaces with real power as you walk among them. No one, I notice, walks within the rectangles, whether out of special regard, superstition, or a fear that they will be stepping on the faces of the dead.

I give Shlomo a wave and he waves back. "Get a load of this," he says with a sweep of his arm. As there are nothing but those empty outlines, I am not sure what he's talking about. Until he points a thumb over his shoulder, and I spot a newer building I somehow hadn't noticed. The structure is off-white, eerily generic, with a lot of old-fashioned windows. It looks designed more for a light industrial park in exurban Cleveland than a torture factory in forties Bavaria. "This is the reconstructed barracks. Have you been?"

"Have I been? I walked right by and didn't even notice the place."

Shlomo tilts his liver-spotted head and squints at me. "Sometimes I worry about you, kiddo."

Then we're inside. And he's shaking his head at something else. I can't blame him. "Do you believe this?" he asks.

What I'm looking at—hard to remember this is a concentration camp—is an enormous airy room, high-ceilinged, featuring deep-polished mahogany-looking tables arranged in a common area, flanked by beautiful handcrafted lockers.

The lockers gleam the same polished red-brown as those tables, each with a nice little slot on top, for the inmates to put their name in.

"It's preposterous," Shlomo says. "You think that when a gang of Soviet POWs came marching in, or a batch of Jews, the SS gave them name tags?"

"I'm gonna go with no," I say.

"Good guess, Einstein."

With those polished cabinets and the spacious benches, we might as well be in the locker room at Mar-a-Lago. I wouldn't be surprised if a waiter showed up to ask if I want a Tom Collins. Clearly the reconstructors wanted to send a message to the present about the past. Which may also explain the toilets, lined side by side in perfect symmetry, minus stalls, but higher quality than those in my own home. Same with the sinks. Fixtures fit for Park Slope. You don't think of a Dachau inmate freshening up before bed, or waking up before a day of slave labor, heading to the group bathrooms with a folded towel over their arm, making sure their skin is hydrated. All that's missing are the soap and lotion dispensers, along with a good shampoo/conditioner. The whole building is sparkling clean. The lighting is terrific. The curators go for real—but in most places (outside of the crematorium and shower rooms), not *too* real. All laid out like a well-maintained nightmare. If you didn't know better, you wouldn't think the actual barracks, like the camp itself, were cramped, or foul-smelling, or full of dying, desperate victims who lived with dysentery, oozing sores, and mortal fear.

All of which may explain why Shlomo, with uncharacteristic ire, completely negs on the place. "I'm so mad," he tells me, "I just want to . . . I don't know what."

I've never seen him so intense. Another couple in the fake barracks turn toward us, then look away fast. At least they aren't bickering, like my old friends Bobby and Marla back in the Auschwitz ovens.

Suddenly, I think I see Homburg Man just outside the faux-barracks entrance, but don't want to bail on Shlomo and check. So I stay put, and lay a hand on my friend's shoulder. "You're not going to do anything crazy, are you?"

"Like what?"

"Like, I don't know, turning over some benches, carving your initials in the lockers?"

"Get out of here, you."

"I'm just kidding."

"I'm not, get out of here. I want to think."

The camps do strange things to people. I've seen it. I've felt it. I feel it now. The retroactive pall of awareness. We're all monsters. If not in the moment, at the very least, potentially.

Hands in my pockets, staring at my shoes, I find myself ambling up the camp road, then crunching on the path that leads away from the crematorium, moving through a beautiful green thicket, past memorial after memorial engraved on flat, weathered stones, lying horizontal on the ground. I find a random, undestroyed napkin on which I'd scribbled a few inscriptions:

*Execution range with blood ditch*
*Pistol Range for Execution*
*Ash grave*
*Ashes were stored here*

At Dachau, it is explained, the ashes from the crematoria were simply dumped in back, scattered, or buried in the now bucolic woods all around the place. Trudging up the path, I am gripped by the thought that it's the ashes themselves I'm crunching underfoot.

(Full disclosure: I once had an awful experience with cremains. I was writing a story about the Neptune Society, an organization devoted to cremating clients and then, for a fee, taking what's left of them and dumping them overboard. Also known as "at-sea burial." Don't ask. I just remember being in a small craft on the waters off Catalina, with a father-and-son team eating McDonald's as they worked, and when they emptied the shoebox full of human cremains over the sides, a strong wind came up and blew them back, and small chunks lodged in their Big Macs. As if that wasn't savage enough, I later found out that at the same time I was watching Pop and Junior scarf down at-sea-burial clients, Natalie Wood was being killed in the very waters in which we were sailing. I'm not going to say Robert Wagner did it—but whoever it was, I was out there the same time they were. Unlike my Dachau experience, visiting the murder site decades after the killers fled the premises. Unless there's something the museum isn't telling us, nobody's killed anybody at Dachau since the forties. With scant fanfare, Dad and Son picked what looked like tiny gray kibble and bits out of their burgers and kept on eating. Admittedly, not thoughts you'd want to have anywhere, but least of all here, where ash, for the most compelling of reasons, is nothing less than a holy word. An idea to wrestle with as the path leads across a little bridge over a creek, so rustic and lovely it might have appeared on a Currier and Ives cookie tin; like the bridge you'd take to Grandma's house, if Grandma lived near a concentration camp.)

This whole train of thought is so disturbing, I'm relieved when I suddenly hear the bells. And keep hearing them. For some reason, don't ask, I start counting the rings. And think to myself, *Well, they're going to stop at twelve.* Except when I check my watch—time tends to disappear on the tour—it's actually closer to three o'clock.

Another mystery.

# CHAPTER 26
## *THE MORTAL AGONY*

🚌 🚌 🚌

THE RINGING JUST KEEPS UP. Thirteen, twenty-four, thirty . . . And did I mention? It's LOUD! Actually oppressive. By thirty-seven, something happens to my brain. I'm borderline deaf, and it's borderline deafening. All the humans in view seem to be walking in the same direction, toward the sound, as if—we're up to forty-five, and I'm not thinking straight—called to worship, drawn forward through some magnetic force in the intense and unrelenting clangs.

By fifty-five, bell still ringing painfully in my ears, I'm out of the sylvan glade and on the path to the forbiddingly named Mortal Agony of Christ Chapel. The Agony is a tall and stunning oval structure shaped, disturbingly, like a giant smokestack made of stone, rising out of the earth with a slice taken out of it. Through that opening—the slice—the faithful can enter and pay their respects to the Catholic prisoners who met their agonizing end at Dachau.

Hard to describe the instant shock and impact of the architecture. Something about it. Mounted high above the entrance is a massive, twisted crown, woven from thorns of black iron. Beneath the crown, inside—I take just a peek—is a square stone altar, placed dead center atop three circular steps. The architect, Josef Wiedemann, said that the circular form was intended to symbolize liberation from captivity by Christ. Beautiful thought. And yet . . .

Behind and above that altar, mounted on the wall, is a large, polished wooden cross, but not like any I've ever seen. Vertical and horizontal bars are equal, so it looks more like a plus sign. Later, I'm unable to figure out what this means, and finally give up googling. Halfway down the rabbit hole, however, I stumble on this from OG Stoic Seneca the Younger (4 BC–65 AD), about Roman crucifixion techniques: "Some have their victims with head down to the ground, some impale their private parts . . ." Prompting Seneca to this not-so-stoical observation: "Anyone facing such a death would plead to die rather than mount the cross . . ." From Josephus (AD 37–100) comes more cross talk, more relevant perspective to the subject at hand: "Every day Roman soldiers caught five hundred Jews or more . . . The soldiers, driven by the hatred of the Jews, nailed them to crosses. They nailed them in many different positions, to entertain themselves and to horrify the Jews watching this spectacle from inside the walled city of Jerusalem. In time, the soldiers ran out of wood for crosses, and room for crosses even if they had found more wood."

And this was 1,939 years before Hitler.

The Catholic chapel, we learn, was dedicated in 1960 through the efforts of ex-prisoners, including one, Johannes Neuhäusler, who became auxiliary bishop of Munich. A plaque on the back reminds us that Polish priests were killed here as well. It was the first religious monument built at the site.

A handful of genuine worshippers are already in the chapel.

Before I leave, I wonder, would it be wrong to tap the nearest worshipper on the shoulder, maybe ask what they think about Pope Pius XII, AKA "Hitler's pope"? The one who kept silent about the Holocaust? Famously, when shown irrefutable evidence—including photographs—of the butchery of Jews in Warsaw, the response from Pius was essentially, *Meh.*

I'm not intending to minimize the suffering of Catholics. Hell is hell. It's just . . . is it wrong to mention the trauma that Catholic leaders engendered by their passivity? This church, at Dachau, is dedicated to the mortal agony of Christ. But before my head explodes, can we say a word about the mortal agony of the children Josef Mengele experimented on? Their agony didn't keep the Vatican from helping Doctor Death, along with Adolf Eichmann, Klaus Barbie, and countless other Reichmonsters, escape punishment and wile away their days in sunny South America. (Well, not Eichmann. The Mossad got him.) But all the rest.

Maybe it's me, but it feels like serious chutzpah that the first religious monument at Dachau was not for the religion that Dachau and all its sister camps were constructed to obliterate. But for a religion whose leaders, among other things, did not just enable that obliteration—they helped the obliterators escape punishment.

When I leave—we're past sixty rings—I spot, across a small patch of grass from the entrance, the actual bell, maybe twenty feet off the ground, encased in a stack of trestles. I don't know why I'm surprised that it's not a recording. Nor, for that matter, is there some death camp Quasimodo on hand to ring the thing, which appears to swing back and forth on its own, powered by some force invisible to the naked eye. Mystery within mystery.

I stand in front of the bell, succumbing to the last brainpan-mangling vibrations, the sound which drives all other sounds out of the head, when a fellow chapel visitor, a fortyish woman with the smoldering eyes of midcareer Sophia Loren—in a habit—smiles in my direction. "It will stop now."

"It, Sister?"

"The bell."

To my surprise, it does

Smiling more indulgently, Sister Sophia adds, "The bell rings every day, just before three o'clock."

When I ask, "Why three o'clock?" she looks surprised. "Three is the hour when Christ died on the cross." With that, her look fades to sadness, maybe pity, that a man can get as old as me and still not know what time Christ died. Before I can explain—they didn't teach that at my school—she moves past me, feet seeming to barely touch the ground, into the chapel. And another voice—this one male, gruff, I'm guessing Russian—whispers from very close behind me, "It's not for Christ. It's for the Soviets. POWs. The SS shot more than sixty of us. The memorial is right over there."

*Us?*

I turn, and here he is, a face straight out of a Tarkovsky film—think *Andrei Rublev*—six feet of looming, unalloyed Russo annoyance, pointing to a spot off to our left. This being pre-COVID, I was more menaced by his breath—the eau de blini—than the possibly poison droplets he was spraying my way.

"You didn't see memorial?" he asks.

"There are a lot of memorials," I say, and instantly hate myself. It sounds so insipid, not to mention defensive and guilty, I wish I'd just nodded sympathetically and lied. "Oh yes. I saw. It's a terrible thing,"

This is a man who speaks about Russian POWS—*us*— as if he was slurping borscht with them last week.

"Did you count the rings? More than sixty," he declares. "One for each man. Shot down like dogs."

"More than sixty," I repeat. I had sixty-eight.

The devastation of this particular travesty, amid all the rest, points to an abiding truth. What you mourn may not be what I mourn, but there is something for everybody to lament. Even if, you know, my pain is bigger than your pain . . .

I wonder if the timeless Russian is, like Homburg Man, a ghost remaining earthbound to tell clueless genocide tourists what time it is, or if he is simply another human transformed by this place into a portentous character himself. All I know is, he didn't mention the pope.

But time out. As I write this, in April 2021, a stabbing pain in my stomach pins me to the back of the chair. As if an invisible gnome has snuck up and stabbed me with a knitting needle. That happens. More and more. But— the good news!—the knitting needles are not from that elusive mass on my kidney. Turns out the lump was iffy but benign. Though no sooner did I get that news then it was discovered I had a throbbing kidney stone—apparently in there since at least 2016, when it was noted on an MRI and promptly forgotten. As in, I was never told about it, and continued to have these random, piercing abdominal pains—in front—and stabs of weird, postoperative pain—in back—depending on where my bouncing baby stone had wandered on any given night or day.

Mind you, I'd heard one treatment for this malady was going in through a "ureter" to remove the thing—the pearl in my penile oyster—a prospect I dreaded more than death itself after months of regular urethra violation due to a "mishap" (doctor's words) during back surgery that left my bladder nonfunctional (the word the nurse used was "dead"), the result of me being on the table two extra hours after Dr. Butterfingers sliced a vein that it took two hours to unslice, and I awoke to a tube in my junk and a bag strapped to my thigh. Because, as it was repeatedly put to me, the bladder had basically died, or at least retired. A state of affairs that led to wearing a catheter and learning to empty a portable urine thermos for a couple of months. At the outset of which I was told, by the Top Bladder Man at St. Johns in Santa Monica, I had a fifty-fifty chance of needing to "self-cath" the rest of my life.

*Good times!*

You want to know fear and loathing? Arrange to be told you're going to be a bag man due to either medical malfeasance or "just one of those things"—depending on how you look at it. Could I have sued? Maybe. Did I want to? Maybe not. I had, you see, made a deal with the Cosmos. If She, He, or It would just return the power to urinate, I'd forego litigation. All I wanted was not to have to spend more endless hours in urologists' offices, trying not to scream when comely nursing assistants, male and female, bade me hold still while they inserted tubes up my urethra—or pulled them out—to see if I could go "on my own."

If I could just make it back from that, I told the Universe, then I would let it all slide.

Which, forgive me if I've already mentioned, I did. Make it back. Thanks to a crack urologist at another hospital, Cedars-Sinai, who rescued me from the grips of a nameless butcher carrying two staples encased in a block of plexiglass, explaining how he'd just put these staples inside my "shaft," and—well, it's all kind of a blank after that. I flashed on Mengele, as one does, and switched prostate doctors . . . The prospect of penile stapling was just too gruesome after those months of tube insertions—a procedure I somehow never learned to endure without shrieking.

But hey, it all worked out. The tubes were removed, I live on bagless, and lo, these many months later, my suspicious mass scare has been defused and dialed back to a mere stone-in-the-kidney situation. Which can blow up into unendurable keel-over-in-the-ER pain in the next five minutes, or continue for years to stab and throb in brief bouts of agita, until—Bob's your uncle—it pops out by itself, or the medicos extract or destroy the thing via some other method. Lasers, maybe, or salad tongs. It's a world of possibility.

To enter the Jewish memorial, mere steps away from the Mortal Agony chapel, the supplicant walks down a ramp through an entranceway formed alarmingly—and I assume deliberately—like the slice-of-bread-shaped doors of the crematoria. It's a high-impact conceit: the downward-sloping ramp extending in the same tonguelike fashion as the gurneys protruding from the mouths of all the ovens in all the camps.

That downward slope leads us into what feels like the depths. And there are, in my experience, no lower-feeling depths than those at the camps—while the roof slants upward to a giant white marble menorah, as if in Jewish response to the grotesquely huge eagles and swastikas on display throughout the reich. (Microsoft Word, I'm not going to capitalize "reich" every time, so stop trying. Who's paying you anyway?) The architecture here makes the subtle, or not-so-subtle, point that the symbol of the Jews is still here, while those icons of Nazi might are nowhere to be seen—at least at Dachau. It's the Jewish religion, forever under siege, which has lasted into its third millennium, far longer than the twelve-count-'em-twelve-year thousand-year reich. Though your Wehrmacht gear, thanks to Herr Trump and his thriving white power fanboys, has made a comeback, and regularly shows up at anti-ZOG rallies here in America. Separate issue. (Sort of.)

The Jewish memorial, we learn, was inaugurated on May 7, 1967. The building, designed by Hermann Zvi Guttmann, was constructed from black lava basalt stone. That basalt itself is a rock formed in geologic terror, in the heat and flames of volcanic eruptions, is a living architectural metaphor.

Once inside, the building feels very much like an underground cell, built from ancient stones, the lowest point of which is illuminated through an opening in the ceiling. A vertical column of white marble, set against that old and earthbound stone, extends upward through a small circular opening in the roof. It's a dizzying use of natural light.

As if to say, *We enter into darkness, on faith, and once in the darkness, light from far over our heads offers the hope of escape—if only as smoke that rises and releases into sky* . . . or something.

Profundities abound. But there's no escaping the message the architect has created in this landscape of horror. Even when I was there, I knew I'd have a hard time describing this. As I stagger from the darkness back out into the Bavarian sun, at once gutted and—here's a word I can barely lift—hopeful (a little), I don't even want to ruin it by figuring out why.

Next stop on the Dachau worship tour is the Protestant Church of Reconciliation, which looks like an assemblage of spare parts. A landscape in concrete. (*Landscape in Concrete*, incidentally, being the name of a bizarre and powerful 1963 novel by Austrian-Jewish writer Jakov Lind, the first Nazi-centric fiction I'd ever read. Described by Blake Butler, in his excellent blog, as "the sort of war book that feels more brain-damaged in its essence than simply cold." A book I also mention because it never made more sense than when I read it again, on the bus. Wheels within wheels.) From a distance this might be a small industrial warehouse or a brutalist motel. It's got odd, random-seeming angles and, I don't know, maybe half a dozen intersecting roofs. This structure, like the Catholic and Jewish ones, manages to be at once stunning and disturbing. Disturbing, in this case, because—well, I'll get to that.

Whatever the effect, you have to admire the effort, on the part of the architect, to find a way to communicate the suffering of this place. Of course, at the time of the Final Solution, lucky for them, Protestants were not the ones being finalized. They were suffering from war—not weaponized genocide.

I'm no expert, but you might call building a concentration camp memorial for a group who were not, themselves, the target of mass killing more like a Holocaust participation prize. But should the number of Protestants who were killed even *be* a criterion? Who the fuck do I think I am? As my old friend Hubert Selby Jr. used to say, you can't compare pain. Speaking of which, Jehovah's Witnesses, whose religion forbade them from saluting Hitler—an edict, amazingly, followers had the strength and faith to honor—were rounded up in droves. But no memorial chapel for them.

Never mind. Helmut Striffler, the architect, has said in interviews that he designed the church to represent a counterpoint to the symmetrical, angular structures and layout of the former camp. (Take the guy at his word, and you can imagine him hunched over the drafting table, making every scribble and blip a fuck-you to the orderly, right-angle-centric fascists in charge. The problem is, saying fuck you in 1967 is a little late. But still . . .) The architect has also explained how he built the Dachau church half underground, as a gesture of humility.

Just one man's opinion, but if guilt dictated depth, Herr Striffler should have built his little chapel a mile underground, like the Pentagon bunker in *Dr. Strangelove*.

Inside the church, you'll find four pews, an actual organ—painted green—and a podium on a column, topped (unless I'm hallucinating) with a Bible on a little stand.

Behind that, to one side, is a circular altar. All made of concrete. All at odd angles and distances from each other, as if positioned to convey alienation from (not connection with) a divine being. The architectural message, to me, is, *I shouldn't be here. But I am. And I am massively uncomfortable.* Though I could be projecting . . .

There is also a steel gate in the chapel created by artist Fritz Kühn and inscribed with words from the seventeenth psalm: "Hide me under the shadow of thy wings." Not to beat a dead German shepherd, but all l can think is, from a certain angle, if you were a Protestant under Hitler you probably *should* hide, from shame. To quote Donald L. Niewyk, whose book *The Jews in Weimar Germany* chronicles (among other things) the depths of pre-Nazi Germanic Jew-hate: the old anti-Semitism had "created a climate in which the 'new' anti-Semitism was, at the very least, acceptable to millions of Germans."

Oh that academic understatement! You might call Martin Luther—the definitive old anti-Semite—a fluffer for Hitler's genocidal money-shots. Though you may be insulting fluffers. Four hundred years before the Third Reich, in *On the Jews and Their Lies* (snappy title!), Germany's fave theologian described Hebrews thusly: "a base, whoring people . . . full of the devil's feces . . . which they wallow in like swine." He went on to advocate that synagogues and Jewish schools be burned, prayer books destroyed, homes torn down, etc. Who knew that back in Reformation days, Martin Luther was composing an SS instruction manual?

So there's that.

Does it bear repeating—danke, Luther!—had German

Christians opposed the Third Reich, there wouldn't have been one? Like it or not, Germany was ready and waiting for the future führer. (Just like America, generations down the road, was fertile turf for a certain stealthily diapered strongman wannabe.)

All of which—stay with me—makes the courage of a cleric like Dietrich Bonhoeffer, who not only opposed Hitler but took part in a plot to kill him, even more profound—especially when you consider what the rest of his peers we're doing.

Just because I can't let it go, here's an item retrieved for the ages on the educational website Facing History. It's from Ludwig Müller, a "Reich Bishop," summing up his German Christian contemporaries' stance toward all things Semitic. "The eternal God created for our nation a law that is peculiar to its own kind. It took shape in the Leader Adolf Hitler, and the National Socialist state created by him . . . One Nation! One God! One Reich! One Church!"

(All I can think of, when I read this, is that photo of evangelicals laying hands on Trump in the Oval Office, when he, too, was declared God's ordained facilitator. But I really have to stop going there.)

Best to stick with Germans and Jesus. Speaking of— concerned with fighting Jewish influence, top-dog Reich-Christers like Herr Müller even banned the Old Testament. Goodbye, Moses.

I've got to get out of here.

# CHAPTER 27
## COMPASSION PORTAL

🚌 🚌 🚌

FROM EARLIER JAUNTS, I already have my death camp refrigerator magnet, and a handful of Auschwitz postcards—who doesn't want to see *Arbeit Macht Frei* on their fridge?—and now I find myself in the final Dachau stop, the obligatory gift shop visit. It's become almost ritual for writers and vloggers to riff on the assorted concentration camp tchotchkes to be had before departing. The usual *I Went to Dachau and All I Got Was This Stupid T-shirt* routine. (I'm kidding. You can't get T-shirts on-site. You can, however, for $19.99, get a "Coordinates of Dachau" tee on Amazon. Black, with *DACHAU* in white, over *GERMANY* in green, over a topographical map with the coordinates in green below: *48.2630° N, 11.4339° E*.)

If you're a person of conscience and don't want to shop Amazon—some might call Mr. Bezos's venture a distant watered-down cousin to slave camps—you can go to the worldclasstees.com, and get your *Straight Outta Dachau* T-shirt for $12.99. Described by the vendors as a "Grunge parody T-shirt."

But we're better than that. Or at least, more fatigued. Having babbled my shame-based way through three camps—with outside biz making the shame shamier—

plus the assorted other Holocaust and Holocaust-adjacent locales, I'm finding myself, here at the keyboard, kind of . . . done. Sundowning at noon.

Do they have Judaica at the Dachau gift shop? Yes. Do they have, oh, I don't know, birthday cards? Of course. Mezuzahs, menorahs, items that let you know they're not marketing to the 4-H Club in Omaha?

Absolutely.

In fact, when I bump into the Omaha ladies in the Dachau bookshop, Pam asks what the mezuzah actually is. I tell her it's a scroll of parchment with twenty-two lines from Deuteronomy, handwritten by a scribe on the skin of a kosher animal, then rolled and squeezed into a tiny, hollow object and mounted outside the door of your home. That old routine (the skin parchment, redolent of Ilse Koch's skin obsession, is part of a long tradition. But it's still creepy. Though not as much as if Ilse had been making mezuzahs.) Let's forget that.

Because I was dragged to Sunday school—on Saturdays—as a boy, I actually remember the highlights of the Torah passage, including the dictate from the Almighty: *And thou shalt love the Lord thy God with all thy heart, and with all thy soul, and with all thy might.*

Not to wax all theological but this seems like a lot to ask of a God who allowed His people to suffer the horrors and torments of Dachau in its pre–gift shop years. Yet faith is a personal matter.

According to ancient rabbis, I inform Pam, mezuzahs keep ill fortune away by driving off demons.

"So it's like your Lucky Jews?" she asks.

Exactly!

Back on the bus after buying them in Warsaw, I'd shown the ladies the little wooden fellows. And hearing her put it this way—I confess, I have to agree: mezuzahs *are* kind of like Lucky Jews, superstition-wise. Except that Lucky Jews are usually owned by non-Jews; mezuzahs, almost always by Jews. At least until Pam and Trudy are turned on to them. In my own small way, I like to think, I'm doing my bit to spread ecumenical good will to the Midwest. Both ladies agree the items sound "kind of neat," and pick up a couple.

The Dachau bookshop, not surprisingly, also carries books that show up on Goodreads' popular Holocaust reading list, and Amazon's 100 best sellers for "Jewish Holocaust History"—all these, plus the movies, docs, and Shoah series you'd expect. The real head-scratcher, for this Semite, are some of the non-Holocaust-specific titles. What, exactly, was the thinking behind bios of esteemed characters like Sigmund Freud, Woody Allen, and Philip Roth? (Well, ex-esteemed, in the case of Allen.) *Selection* is a loaded word in the world of camps, but why were these Jews selected? Is this the memorial equivalent of saying all's forgiven—turns out, some of those Jews are darn impressive, and real yuck-hucksters!

While burning Freud's books, young Nazis recited a "fire oath" about "the soul-shredding overvaluation of sexual activity." Which, besides making Nazis sound like the world's first incels, is an incantation the young fascists could have could have reused with Allen and Roth, had the pair been born a generation or two earlier.

And what about those names the Dachau shop doesn't

include? No knock on this illustrious trio, but had they been searching for celebrity Jews in the battle against Nazism, memorial overseers might have widened the net and included Moe Howard, who was the first to parody Adolf Hitler—as the leader of Moronika, in the *Three Stooges* short *You Nazty Spy!*—a full nine months before Chaplin showed up as the Great Dictator. In *Nazty*, Brother Curly filled out the role of Hermann Göring, "Field Marshal Gallstone," and Larry portrayed a Goebbels-like minister of propaganda. (Chaplin, in his autobiography, said he would not have made *Dictator* had he known about the concentration camps. More food for thought.)

Innocuous as it seems now, Moe, Larry, and Curly had to suffer the not inconsiderable wrath of isolationist senators Burton Wheeler and Gerald Nye (who sound like characters from the TV show), furious that the Stooges were, by their lights, trying to mobilize the country for war with anti-Nazi propaganda.

No question the ex-vaudeville trio were less respectable than the Prestige Jew Club of Freud, Einstein, and Roth. Which may be the same reason, despite their bone-deep Jewishness, the Dachau managers left out Lenny Bruce, Larry David, or for that matter, Sarah Silverman, who's done one of the most classic Holocaust jokes of all time. Talking about when her niece called her up to tell her how she'd learned in Hebrew school that Nazis killed sixty million Jews, the comedienne explained, "I corrected her, and I said, 'You know, I think he's responsible for killing *six* million Jews.' And she says, 'Oh yeah, six million. I knew that. But seriously, auntie, what's the difference?' 'The difference is that sixty million is unforgivable.'"

Too soon?

Maybe. But if I had Bill Gates money, I'd promise a donation to the memorial, and make it contingent on including this joke.

Some, certainly, would call any kind of commercialization at the memorial disrespectful to survivors and their families. Understandable. But once again, isn't the presence of a Jewish gewgaw and book outlet more evidence that the torturers lost? It's not like Dachau's administrators toss in *Mein Kampf* and wash-off swastika tats alongside the dreidels.

At what point marketing merges into disrespect may be a personal issue. In 1993, McDonald's was lambasted for distributing flyers advertising their new camp-convenient franchise in the Dachau parking lot. During my visit, decades later, there are no locals passing out circulars for Mickey D's. For that matter, there are still no billboards in the crematorium.

There are plenty of movie theaters in the Dachau area, and the ovens are as good a place as any for coming attractions. With the rise in neo-Nazism in Germany and the rest of the continent, it may be the best place of all.

The gruesome truth, in the semi-sterile confines of Dachau, is that the truth does not appear entirely gruesome. Or maybe not gruesome enough.

Not as gruesome, at any rate, a few years after my camp visits, in 2021, when comparisons between the torments of the Holocaust and the torment of restrictions engendered to combat COVID became de rigueur.

Does it mean anything, by the time you read this (can we, at this point, just go with BTTYRT?), that a Republican county chairman had to apologize for posting a Holocaust cartoon on his Facebook page, marching out the Six Million to mock Kansas Governor Laura Kelly's mask mandate? The caption reads: "Lockdown Laura says: Put on your mask . . . and step onto the cattle car."

Then again, after the random end-times Trump day, January 6, 2021, when rioting MAGAs stormed the Capitol for the sheer seditious joy of (among other things) plopping an ass in Nancy Pelosi's desk chair, or dropping a deuce and stomping it in the congressional carpet, does right-wing cattle-car humor even merit a raised eyebrow? Given that the tees and hoodies of choice for Trump's fecal lynch mob bore chuckly logos like *Camp Auschwitz*, the answer is probably no. Where are the Lucky Jews when you need them?

Anti-Semitic fashion aside, I would like to think that the pain and suffering of the Holocaust and what we feel, confronted with it, can be a portal to ongoing agonies suffered by others. Be it plague, poverty, racial injustice, sexual abuse, bigotry, global warming, being unhoused, and on and on and on—it all happened, it never stops happening. You cannot compare pain. But you can have compassion, you can embrace the responsibility of doing something, anything, to comprehend and combat the horror that while not, overtly, yours, undeniably *is*. You can, by walking the topography of blood and screams, transform the abstract to the visceral. And do something.

You can, at least, if you're a better person than me.

Obviously, the Holocaust of the 1940s is done; but the ongoing genocide-adjacent assault on human rights—globally, locally, nationally—continues. And speaking only for myself, I will say that on this trip I wanted to feel something, desperately. And perhaps because of this pressure, this sense of needing to Gandhi-morph, sprout wings, and ascend to lofty heights of camp-inspired love, I felt nothing. Or a kind of nothing. A temporary, let's say, overwhelming emptiness. And thought that if I ever needed it, proof of my sociopathic nature was now at hand. It was just TOO MUCH. Until I realized—cheap paradox department—feeling overwhelmed and feeling nothing are not that different. Both, perhaps, evidence, or result, of all the garbage culture we absorb, all the self-obsessed trivialities that can, at any given time, crowd out meaning— crowd out history—numbed by earbuds, screens, the non-stop curdle of current events. On some days, I hope you can't relate, work exists as the moments between checking the phone and dabbing CNN. For something. Anything. And yet . . .

Since returning from Germany, I have, while driving, flashed frequently on the camp—the hair, the shoes, the outsized eyes of soon-to-die children—and caught myself drifting into oncoming traffic, as abstracted as a beer drunk after fifteen Schlitz.

We are wired how we're wired. In my case, to believe in nothing. And yet, I would say to me (if we were speaking), you can't unsee what you saw. And from that vision, out of it, moving forward, I only know that some switch has been turned.

Of course, self-hate and self-obsession are always there, like some drooly, exhausting dog you feed by the accident of merely breathing. But that doesn't mean you devote your life to making Rover huge.

I know, for example, that for years I thought I'd used heroin not to feel. Until it hit me, writing this, that the truth may be even less ennobling: that perhaps I used it to mask the truth that I did not feel at all. I just wanted to. Or needed a reason. Or something . . .

Every day, for months, I have sat down at the comfortable yet guaranteed-to-cause-a-spine-ache chair in which I type, staring at the coffee-stained screen, tapping the sticky keyboard, to reach some kind of final thought. To have that Big On-the-Page Moment. *SAD!* as a former president might say.

Then again, I have read that next to airplane headrests and public toilets, there is nothing germier than personal keyboards. Which is a separate issue—or not. We bring our germs to the party. But before the metaphor crumbles under the strain, perhaps the effect of exposing oneself to the physical scenes of Holocaust is not unlike the method our dear departed leader once suggested could clear up infections. Is history the bleach we can ingest? Is exposure to genocidal darkness a source of illumination, like the light Donald Trump wanted to insert rectally to sanitize our parts? To, essentially, save us?

All I know, since returning from Eastern Europe, since deboarding that "luxury coach," is that I have never loved my children—and feared my neighbors, my country, and my century—more. I have, in short, internalized the possibilities implicit in every stinging detail of Dachau, Buchenwald, and Auschwitz.

And I'll tell you, I don't care if the Holocaust is, in the eyes of some, an industry. I don't care that whole swaths of the camps have been recreated into ersatz tableaux, I don't care if you can buy a slice after the crematorium and wash it down with Fanta. Nothing, in the end, can diminish the searing gravitas of the physical place on which the martyrs, our ancestors, walked. On which, as Yahweh (or Eichmann) intended, we experience the vigorous, well-earned, necessary despair of confronting humanity at its worst—of seeing our own reflection in the hellhouse mirror.

Call it the redemption of the living by the dead.

That is the gift. That is the horror. That, in the end, is the only reality that matters.

My message of hope—and obligatory (if questionably) redemptive antidepression—is that the Holocaust was not an exception. It is the time between holocausts that is the exception. So savor these moments.

Be grateful. Even if the ax is always falling.

**The End**

## Acknowledgments

The author is grateful to the following for their help, editorial and otherwise: Marc Maron, Eric Bogosian, Lydia Lunch, Stephen Sayadian, Johnny Temple, Aaron Petrovich, Johanna Ingalls, Susannah Lawrence, Khadijah Mitchell, Sohrab Habibion, Jonathan Smith, Adele Bertei, Allen Michelson, David Breithaupt, Jeff Feuerzeig, Tyler Waxman, Mary Landre, and Robert Downey Jr.

Thanks, as well, to Danny Gabai and *Vice*, where some of this material appeared in an earlier form.

*In memory of Stuart Cornfeld*
*(November 13, 1952–June 26, 2020)*

A CONVERSATION BETWEEN
BEN STILLER AND JERRY STAHL
ABOUT *NEIN, NEIN, NEIN!*

🚌 🚌 🚌

**Ben Stiller:** Where did you come up with this million-dollar idea?

**Jerry Stahl:** I was very depressed, and I realized I was also a Jew. So, I wanted to go somewhere where being a depressed Jewish person and in total despair were completely appropriate.

**Stiller:** Right.

**Stahl:** And where better than over at the camps, at the site of the camps? And I got *Vice Magazine* to do a six-part series where they let me cover the sort of Holocaust-tourism angle. But what made it special was that it was by bus. It was a bus tour with people I did not know. Many from the Midwest, and some who had never seen a Jew.

**Stiller:** And how did it work out?

**Stahl:** They've now seen a Jew. You know, it was awkward at first, but I grew to like them.

**Stiller:** The book is really good. I think it's some of your best work, one of your best books. You are uniquely a person who is willing to go to places like this, in terms of finding humor, finding something in there that is probably uncomfortable, but something that is worth excavating. And on the outside, I was like, *Oh gosh, is this book going to be really upsetting, depressing?* and I found it very . . . First of all, it's a page-turner. It really is. And it starts out that you have all these observations of all these people who are from different places. And seem kind of like these characters that you're not going to connect with, but I felt by the end of the book that there is a connection you have with each of them in some way, and it's very moving. Because of this process that you go through with them. And the experience you have with them, but not in a forced sort of way. And then the actual experience of going to each of these camps and these different places that have such a heavy history and heavy meaning, and the challenge that you put in front of yourself to write something about this that hasn't been written before.

**Stahl:** That is the challenge with everything. But I think the thing that makes this book a little different is it . . . look, the Holocaust is the Holocaust. So what I wrote about is the experience, the humanity of it. You're dealing with people who are going to see the ovens, then strolling out and having a slice at the Auschwitz snack bar. And that is the element where some of the humor and the weirdness comes in. It's just, who knew? Or the Auschwitz men's room attendant, who I figure is like fourth-generation crapper hand. Did his great-grandfather help Himmler?

**Stiller:** It starts out, *Oh, that's a funny observation,* but then you really get into it and go there and start to explore, like what is the reality for the Auschwitz men's room attendant. You talked to him, right?

**Stahl:** I tried to talk to him. He didn't take a shine to me. And I could never figure out—because it seems like the only booming segment of the Polish economy is the toilet sector. You can't go to the bathroom in Poland without having to put money in like a little bowl with a guy sitting there. I could never figure out if you paid on the way in or the way out. So, I paid twice. And he *still* didn't like me.

**Stiller:** When I go to a restaurant that has a men's room attendant, I always feel bad because I usually don't bring my wallet and then I feel guilty.

**Stahl:** They think you're chiseling.

**Stiller:** I don't pay on either side.

**Stahl:** You can't win.

**Stiller:** And I wondered, you know, when you're in there and you're experiencing this and you're writing about it . . . what are you thinking as you're in there? Are you thinking, *I'm going to figure out, I'm going to write about this*? Did you have a plan as to what the book was going to say? Because I think the observation of it is so effective because it makes you think, *How do we process these horrible things that* *happened?* And as an observer, as a tourist, you get disconnected from the actual humanity of the experience.

**Stahl:** You do get disconnected from the humanity, but also on some profound level that makes it more human. That people are going there in their *I'm with Stupid* T-shirts, and their Saturday-at–Disney World little red shorts. It's easy to be judgmental. I think the art of it, to the extent there is any, is finding a way to connect with these people. When I was younger, I just used to make fun of people, and then as I got older, I realized how lame that was. I don't know how it is when you're shooting or acting in a scene. Do you always know consciously where you're going, or does it sort of emerge and you kind of surprise yourself? Because that's how it is with me when I write. It's like, *Wow, I didn't know I was going to go there.*

**Stiller:** Yeah. I think that hopefully when you're in process with something, you're not that aware of what your end result is going to be. That's where you want to be. Sometimes you're *too* aware of that. But as you were there going through this experience, and as you were visiting each camp, were you thinking about what it was all going to amount to?

**Stahl:** Absolutely not. I was just trying to get through the next five minutes.

**Stiller:** Right.

**Stahl:** I mean, the first thing that happened to me at Auschwitz, and this is a mortifying thing to say, is I got sunburned. So, I'm sitting in line at Auschwitz waiting for the ticket and my neck gets sunburned, and I'm feeling all crabby that I got a burn, like I went to Auschwitz and got *burned*, essentially. I kind of hated myself for having that thought. But on one level you can't disconnect the human element of going there . . . you just can't deny that. You want to go and have this profound, deep feeling, and on some level, it occurred to me, there was no emotion you could, it's almost an insult to the dead, to think you can appropriately feel exactly something worthy of what they went through. Does that make sense?

**Stiller:** Sure, yeah. And, also, wasn't it at Buchenwald that you ran into a plate-glass window at the cafeteria?

**Stahl:** I did. I walked into a plate-glass window after walking through the cafeteria very judgmentally, kind of like, *Look at you fucking people, how dare you have blintzes after, you know* . . . and then I walked into a plate-glass window and had to go skulking back past them, bleeding from my forehead, to go to the men's room and get some wet paper towels. So, I think there's a lesson there.

**Stiller:** It's really, really interesting to me because I feel like what you experience in the book is grappling with how we as people are supposed to deal with stuff like this. And also, you don't tell us what we're supposed to feel. And I was thinking, how long did it take you to know when it was the end? Because I imagine, you write this whole experience . . . did you feel a need to somehow summarize or have some sort of lesson or moral? When did you know you were finished writing the book?

**Stahl:** It took me years to get this book going because there was shit happening in my life, you know, which is part of the book.

**Stiller:** This brings me back to the epigraph at the front of the book from a Romanian philosopher, E.M. Cioran. This epigraph, to me, is basically you as a writer in a nutshell, and it says, "*Write books only if you are going to say in them the things you would never dare confide to anyone.*" I feel like as a writer, you're fearless that way. You open yourself up. That's what *Permanent Midnight* is, and *OG Dad*. Can you really do that and live with those consequences? And how has that been for you?

**Stahl:** Look, I'm not an *advice* kind of guy, but there was a great writer I interviewed many years ago named Bruce Jay Friedman, a Jewish American writer, and he said if you write a sentence that makes you squirm, keep going. And I've sort of been squirmy ever since I got that advice. You know, you squirm your way through the book. I think you kind of have to make it hot for yourself, because if you don't say something that's dangerous, then what the fuck, what business do you have writing anything? I also had a question simultaneous with this: how soon after arriving at a death camp did all the normal problems that people have in their life—their love life, their career, their marriage, their status, their successes and failures, meeting the mortgage, do their kids like them, do their kids love them, you know, all this normal stuff—how soon does that dissipate and you're just dealing with survival?

**Stiller:** Yeah, because these were all people just living their lives.

**Stahl:** You're going through your shit and there you are at Auschwitz, and should you suddenly just think appropriate thoughts? Or are you still dealing with all of the stuff that followed you there, you know what I mean?

**Stiller:** Yeah, that is such a valid question. That's what so many people have had to deal with. You know, I do work with refugees.

**Stahl:** I know you do, yeah.

**Stiller:** I think right now there are over a hundred million displaced people in the world. People displaced out of their homes by no fault of their own.

Some due to war. It could be any one of us that something like that could happen to. And in a way we want to disconnect from that.

**Stahl:** It's easy to keep things abstract. And I think the genius and the real value among other values that you do is you humanize these people, and I've seen you go talk to people about their lives. As if they're real people and not statistics, and that's invaluable.

**Stiller:** Yeah, like Auschwitz has a Twitter feed where they just put up the names and pictures of different people who were lost in the camp. It shows you a picture of them in their life before they were in the camp, and what they did, and who their family was, and it's really disturbing because you see it's not just something you can disconnect from.

**Stahl:** So, I look at that and then I press *Like*.

**Stiller:** That's right.

**Stahl:** I don't think that's the heaviest thing you can do. But it's the option you're given. Or you retweet sometimes if you're particularly moved.

**Stiller:** It's a weird thing. What is that? It's connected to social media activism, and what does that really mean? But yeah, how do you "like" a picture from Auschwitz?

**Stahl:** Exactly. But how do you *not?* You press the little heart.

**Stiller:** I think it's when you're at Dachau where you talk about how the ashes of the burned victims were just dumped out. And so, where you're walking around, you're walking around literally on the ashes . . .

**Stahl:** You can't help but think that you are treading on the bones and ash of the dead. And it's one of those living metaphors, because where are you going to walk? Where else *can* you walk? But it's literally on the ashes of the dead and it is not a comfortable thought, but it's an unavoidable one.

**Stiller:** And it's inescapable.

**Stahl:** Exactly.

**Stiller:** The way you describe it, basically, being there is going to affect you in a way you can't really get away from. Even thinking about this talk and having read the book, I had a weird dream about a concentration camp.

**Stahl:** What was the dream?

**Stiller:** I don't know. It was . . . I don't remember it exactly, but I remember waking up and thinking about a concentration camp, and I was thinking, *God, I'm having this reaction just having read your book, let alone what would be the reaction of having gone there and visited all of these places. Let alone what would be the reaction of my life if I had lived through it or had . . .* It's a very heavy thing.

**Stahl:** The thought that plagued me is that as a writer or artist of any kind, are you even worthy to write this? So, what I focused on is not what everybody else focuses on—the truly heavy import and historical resonance—but about the real sort of everyday weirdness of humanity going to see the worst of humanity.

**Stiller:** Did you need time to process it?

**Stahl:** There was a lot of stuff going on in my life and there was a lot of hesitation about the subject, and finally, I don't have a lot of discipline as a writer. I have to engineer it so that the only thing more uncomfortable than writing is *not* writing. And when I get to that point—

**Stiller:** You push yourself.

**Stahl:** I start writing. Because it's better than the alternative.

**Stiller:** So, this took a while. Was it interesting to have the perspective of a few years?

**Stahl:** Yeah, it absolutely was. And plus, another thing happened which was . . . I won't bore you with the details, but for reasons almost too ridiculous to enunciate, all my notes were disappeared. So, I had to sort of remember as much as I could. I'm one of these people who buys notebooks, and by the end I'm writing on the back of receipts and moldy little napkins and scribbling on airplane tickets, and that's where all the stuff is and somehow that got dumped. A friend of mine's grandmother needed work and I said, "I'm not a guy who has maids, but here, why don't you come over and clean up my place?" And she of course saw this pile of scribbled-on crap and threw it out.

**Stiller:** Oh God.

**Stahl:** So that happened. Which might have been the best thing that ever happened. There's that great Oliver Sacks quote, which I'm absolutely butchering, but basically, *Memory is the stories we tell ourselves about what we* think *happened.*

**Stiller:** You're kind of remembering memories.

**Stahl:** I was remembering. I was inventing the story of that trip disguised as what I thought was memory. If that makes any sense. And then there was, throw Trump in the mix, because at the same time while I was there, you know, Trump was happening. So, I had all these truly earthshaking revelations and comparisons about Trump and Hitler, which of course are completely stale by the time I start writing the book. But the only one that matters is that Hitler was an assclown too, a lot of people don't realize. People didn't take him seriously. They thought he was ridiculous.

**Stiller:** It's interesting because growing up Jewish in New York, I never experienced anti-Semitism. Total bubble of being a kid.

**Stahl:** Really? I so envy that.

**Stiller:** And you grew up in Pittsburgh.

**Stahl:** Yeah, I grew up in Pittsburgh. Not to brag. And I went to a grade school of like eight hundred and I was pretty much the only Jew. So, I mean, I was routinely accused of killing Christ.

**Stiller:** How would you—

**Stahl:** Which I must have done during a blackout at the age of five.

**Stiller:** You have that guilty look.

**Stahl:** Once you say, "I didn't do it," you look even guiltier. It's flypaper. You can't win.

**Stiller:** You talk about your dad growing up in Pittsburgh. There's something I didn't know about your dad that you have in the book—I didn't realize he was a refugee.

**Stahl:** Yes, he came over from Lithuania. Well, actually, about three weeks ago I found out he was born in Ukraine; my sister told me. But he came over from Lithuania. It's kind of a tragic story, but to make it fast: his mother married a distant cousin and came over here, but that cousin would not pay for him, so he was two and she had to abandon him, and eight years later she worked in the guy's grocery store and made enough money to send for him. And he would never talk about it.

**Stiller:** So, he lived in a little town . . .

**Stahl:** He moved to a little coal town in Pennsylvania when he came over here. He had lived in some village in Lithuania and all he would ever say about it was, "We were the only family that didn't have a cow." Which is one of the saddest things I've ever heard.

**Stiller:** Probably felt better when he came over here—

**Stahl:** Everybody had a cow.

**Stiller:** Or *didn't* have a cow.

**Stahl:** Cows aplenty.

**Stiller:** But your dad was a judge, right?

**Stahl:** Yeah, he had an amazing story. Came from nothing, and worked his way up. He was attorney general of Pennsylvania.

**Stiller:** He was attorney general of the *state*?

**Stahl:** He was for a while, yeah. He was on the circuit court briefly, for about a year and a half, until one morning he—there's no other way to say this—they found him in the front seat of the Olds with the motor running and the garage door down, and that was that.

**Stiller:** And you've written about that?

**Stahl:** Yeah, I've written about that.

**Stiller:** Obviously, that's a huge thing for anybody to have to go through. Up to that point, what I hadn't known about your dad was that he'd gone through that refugee experience. You said he had a lot of rage and anger.

**Stahl:** Very subdued.

**Stiller:** Suppressed.

**Stahl:** Suppressed. He was a very gentle guy. By the way, at Ellis Island the name was *Stalinsky* and they chopped it off, strangely. Just an irrelevant fact. How different life would have been.

**Stiller:** Stalinsky?

**Stahl:** Yeah, Stalinsky. It's a whole other world I would have had.

**Stiller:** They could have cut it off at *Stalin*.

**Stahl:** Also, when I was growing up . . . I'm about ten years older than you. It was bad enough being a Jew, but then if they thought you were *Russian*, in the fifties and sixties, it was bad news. Like, "Hey Stalin, why don't you go back to Moscow . . ." I had it going and coming in grade school. That said, of course, other people have it a million times worse. This is just *my* story.

**Stiller:** Right. But *everybody's* story is their own story. And that's definitely a heavy thing that you had to deal with. And it obviously shaped a lot of your childhood, I would imagine.

**Stahl:** My father never said a word about it, but in an unspoken way, I always felt tremendously guilty that I had it so easy compared to what he went through. He had a mysterious scar down his left elbow. And wouldn't talk about it. You know, just like, "Stuff happened." Worked in a bottle factory as a kid, and somehow it's just, I don't know. It was a mystery, and sadly, I never got to hear.

**Stiller:** I had a sort of different version of that, because my dad grew up on the Lower East Side, and I think he went through a lot, because he grew up very poor too. But he was first-generation—

**Stahl:** Was his father a bus driver?

**Stiller:** His father was a bus driver and a cabdriver. I don't know what your relationship was like with your dad, but our dad didn't want us to know, he just wanted . . .

**Stahl:** Isn't that interesting.

**Stiller:** He was very loving and supportive.

**Stahl:** He didn't want you to know how hard he had it.

**Stiller:** I think he had his own suppressed rage too, but that came out also as an actor, in his work. Like in a funny way.

**Stahl:** And thank God it did.

**Stiller:** It was part of what his whole thing was. It

was really all in there. But I feel like for you, you developed this sort of persona as a tough guy—the tough, cool, druggie, writer guy—when you were younger.

**Stahl:** I think the key word is *persona*.

**Stiller:** But I've seen pictures of you in the seventies, and you had hair like a big Jewfro sort of thing.

**Stahl:** There was the Jewfro period. But it's hard to look tough when you have a Jewfro.

**Stiller:** But you did. You looked cool. You had a thing going on. And I was asking earlier why you have that persona, or *had* that persona? Why did you develop that?

**Stahl:** Well, I think anybody who has to look tough is operating from a place of complete fear. I was telling you how back in the junkie days—and I am contractually obliged to mention heroin in every interview, so I don't want to violate that, but you know . . .

**Stiller:** You have a deal with heroin?

**Stahl:** I have a deal with heroin.

**Stiller:** Heroin royalties?

**Stahl:** It's a product-placement thing. I was going

to hold something up, but we don't want a Lenny Bruce situation. Whatever that means. So yeah, I had a front. I had a great front, a tough front. With absolutely nothing behind it.

**Stiller:** But you had your writing style. When did you develop this amazing prose style?

**Stahl:** Well, very kind of you, but most of my work was as a journalist, pre-Internet. It's like a decade and half never happened because it never got digitized. So, I started as a feature magazine writer. There's that pulp kind of dictum that you always start at the moment of highest action. With feature magazines, I was trying to grab people by the collar. I would spend three weeks on the first sentence, then write the fucking thing in, like, a day.

**Stiller:** Just figuring out where the jumping-off point is. But there was a lot of pressure from editors. That you have to write something to . . .

**Stahl:** That people want to read.

*This is an edited excerpt of a conversation between Ben Stiller and Jerry Stahl at the 92nd Street Y, New York, on October 12, 2022. To see a video of the full conversation, visit www.92ny. org/archives/jerry-stahl-and-ben-stiller. Special thanks to the 92nd Street Y.*

*Ben Stiller is an award-winning actor, director, writer, and producer. His acting credits include* Meet the Parents, Night at the Museum, The Royal Tenenbaums, The Meyerowitz Stories, *and* While We're Young. *Inspired by a visit to Haiti in 2009 alongside the organization Save the Children, Stiller founded the Stiller Foundation, a nonprofit that provides funds, resources, and support in the rebuilding of schools and educational programs in Haiti. For his considerable philanthropic work amid an illustrious career, Stiller was recognized in 2010 by* TIME *as one of the* TIME *100, a list of the world's most influential people.*